FRENCH TRAGEDY

Books by Albert Cook

THE DARK VOYAGE AND THE GOLDEN MEAN
THE MEANING OF FICTION
OEDIPUS REX: A MIRROR FOR GREEK DRAMA
PROGRESSIONS (poems)
THE ODYSSEY (verse translation)
THE CLASSIC LINE: A STUDY IN EPIC POETRY
PRISMS: STUDIES IN MODERN LITERATURE
THE ROOT OF THE THING: THE BOOK OF JOB AND
    THE SONG OF SONGS
THE CHARGES (poems)
ADAPT THE LIVING (poems)
ENACTMENT: GREEK TRAGEDY
SHAKESPEARE'S ENACTMENT: THE DYNAMICS OF
    RENAISSANCE THEATRE
FRENCH TRAGEDY: THE POWER OF ENACTMENT
MYTH AND LANGUAGE

FRENCH TRAGEDY:
THE POWER
OF ENACTMENT

ALBERT COOK

Swallow Press
Ohio University Press
Chicago   Athens, Ohio   London

Swallow Press Books are published by
Ohio University Press, Athens, Ohio

Library of Congress Cataloging in Publication Data

Cook, Albert Spaulding.
  French tragedy.

  Includes bibliographical references.
  1. French drama (Tragedy)—History and criticism.
2. French drama—17th century—History and
criticism. 3. Racine, Jean Baptiste, 1639–1699—
Criticism. and interpretation. 4. Corneille,
Pierre, 1606–1684—Criticism and interpretation.
I. Title.

PQ61.C6   842'.4'09   80–39611
ISBN 0-8040-0548-6 (Swallow Press: v. 3)

TO THE POETS OF BUFFALO

CONTENTS

PREFACE

Role playing perfuses the life, the lives, we live. There is even a felt gain when two persons can suffuse a mutual awareness of role playing with some leaven of witty reference to the fact. At moments we gather and focus the role playing to some deep common reference: we partake in ritual, a term that may cover as wide a range as the Aztec sacrificial ball game, the Navajo singing rite of healing, the mock battles involving real deaths in New Guinea, and such "civilized" phenomena as school graduations, therapy groups, and official receptions.

Most, if not all, rituals involve not only special rules for the occasion but a kind of framing in space and time.[1] If all the rules are removed but one enjoining relative silence upon auditors who may normally speak, and if the presentation is partly or wholly detached from its social purposiveness, then we have arrived at that strange excrescence of human behavior, the theater.

A line has been drawn that makes for a doubling: what happens on stage resembles some imagining of what happens in life. The actors manipulate their own psychic predispositions; exhibitionism provides a personal gratification for the behavior that gave Rousseau and Diderot pause. And the psychic dispositions of the spectators, when they look on in a way otherwise taboo, are likewise called into play. When they leave the theater, ceasing to be spectators, they may imitate, or shun, the behavior on stage, which itself was an imitation.

In either case they do not quite close the circle; nor is the communication taking place across the line between actors and spectators wholly confined to these psychic processes. Not only are identity and difference called into play, both on stage and between characters and spectators. The theater will manipulate the relation *between* identity and difference. As René Girard says, "great theater is necessarily a play of differentiation and undifferentiation."[2]

Ritual, out of which theater rose, differs from theater in being purposive: Dionysus is being worshipped, a person is being healed, rain is being invoked. And the purposiveness of ritual involves a firm set for identity and difference, where theater plays them against one another.

In the purity of its doubling between make-believe and real, theater tends towards the gratuitous, the mere rehearsal of well-known myths and stories, as in the Ramayana cycle of South Indian and Indonesian theaters or our own plays about such people as Lincoln and Churchill. In a thousand ways the gratuitous theater may offer myth-tinged fantasy, such as the Chinese opera or the Grade B movie.

But Sophocles does not merely rehearse the Oedipus story, and he does not merely use myth as a motor for fantasy. Shakespeare does not offer just a live reenactment of pious thoughts about Richard II or Henry IV or even just hold our attention while the king is shown to die. A deep meditation has been mounted, one that enlists all the special features of a given theatrical tradition to transmit its message. The theater has entered the rarefied air of true drama, as has happened perhaps only six times in human history: fifth century Greece, medieval Japan, Renaissance England and France and Spain, and the modern West.

A space is purified and set off for the theatrical presentation, whether a special building for that purpose alone, a structure improvised and transformed for the time of performance, or the disembodied screen whose whiteness works when the space of a room is darkened. Time, too, is cleared for the performance: during this block of hours only theater will happen. In the audience the spectators have paid at least their time to watch, and usually some money too. On stage the presented events suffer a deformation of time as well.

Since the time of the play is both short and self-contained, it may advertise its self-containment by adhering to some version of the unities, as Corneille and Racine do. It may advertise its relation to the real world not only by including, but also by placing strategically, the key events of a personal life cycle, marriage and death. It may advertise its shortness by varying the tempo, as Shakespeare does; by stylized musical interruption, as in the Greek theater; or by the evenness of its progressions, as in Corneille and Racine. The measured verse of the language in nearly all theatrical traditions offers an overdetermination of speech, a time-measurement of speech, that corresponds to the self-containment of the time for the theatrical presentation. Every line reminds us we have only so far to go. Modernist self-awareness produces extravagant manipulations of theatrical time: the lightning-short plays of Beckett, Robert Wilson's nearly imperceptible slow motions alternated with dizzying whirls, the ponderous boredom of nonnarrative in the film of Warhol and others, the flicking speed-up of Jonas Mekas.

In our panoptican repertoire of theatrical possibilities, we have the danced theater of ballet and modern dance, in which the time of music instead of the time of verse controls the tempo of presentation, and moving bodies speak. We have the rigorous self-containment and minimalist muting of the mime performance, where the action must avoid the regularity of dance. And we have the film, disembodied in space and time as we perceive its sequence of images, though we come to the film expecting we will be released into the light after a given segment of our own time.

On the open box of their stage Corneille and Racine, in their different ways, saw the possibility of singlemindedness. Uniformity of style, relative bareness of metaphor, an intensively interactive small cast of characters, and single, extreme action, were made to converge for plays of extreme and exemplary force.

INTRODUCTION

The plays of Racine and Corneille are remarkably reductive, simple and intense. Moreover, in their enactment, these qualities can be derived from one another: reductiveness from simplicity or vice versa, intensity from either. Their success makes them, then, a kind of clear paradigm, or extreme model, for the presentation in drama of a human essence, reductive, simple, and intense. When these plays break suddenly out of the melodrama of their times into the rarefied air of true drama, they reinvest the impulse to profundity not in the diversity of Shakespeare or the complexity of Sophocles, but back into the singleness of an ideal nobility demonstrated under extremes of paradox and loss.

In these plays no opening is provided for anything like an Aristotelian fault, except at momentary falterings. Fault lies in the total condition. The Cid only begins to show the extent of his nobility in the automatic honor by which he challenges his beloved's father to the initial duel, to say nothing of his offstage military heroism. His full nobility becomes manifest only as he offers his own death, first at Chimène's hand and then at her champion's, in ways that allow her to work her way out of the paradox between duty toward her father and love for his killer.

In Racine's most reductive play, in *Bérénice*, three lovers, all noble, all royal, all friends, enact the self-transformations that allow Antiochus, the failed, silenced suitor, first to leave forever, then to refuse to conduct Bérénice home for his friend the successful rival, then to agree never to see her again. Antiochus in the last scene reveals the rivalry that all their nobility had obviated his having to show anyone but the Bérénice whom he had bid eternal farewell in the opening of the play. Now he reveals the project, noble for a Roman, of a sacrifice that will release them from bonds that keep increasing the desperate love:

> *Jamais je ne me suis senti plus amoureux.*
> *Il faut d'autres efforts pour rompre tant de noeuds.*
> (V,7)

> Never have I felt me to be more in love.
> Other efforts are needed to break so many bonds.

The "noeuds" were there for the three in the very beginning; Antiochus only came to Titus' attention in the first place, long before the play, through a backlash-courage over his despair that Bérénice was falling in love with the Roman. Now, at the end, he does not know that his is the last of three suicide projects. Titus has already stopped Bérénice's silent one, when he discovers it, by declaring that he will kill himself if she kills herself.

Death here is not the end of the tragedy. Rather, it serves as a shadow resort for a nobility that gets beyond such immolation: the *princes* are, as Bérénice says in stopping Antiochus, "trop généreux." Instead of dying, they are to go their separate ways, since the Bérénice who eternally loves an eternally loving Titus cannot marry an Antiochus who, loving, cannot himself help fatally knowing this bar. Antiochus, who had seemed equal in generosity, now submits, in final humility, to confirming this lesson from the lovers. His final "Hélas" voices for them what is too deep for them to voice. The aspiration, trans-Roman but not specifically Christian, converges with the exemplum Bérénice herself concludes by declaring that they are to be. (She speaks only to Antiochus, but her speech has a courteous, still more delicate, reverberation of exhortation and declaration to the sorrowing presence of her silent lover Titus.):

Prince, après cet adieu, vous jugez bien vous-même
Que je ne consens pas de quitter ce que j'aime,
Pour aller loin de Rome écouter d'autres voeux.
Vivez, et faites-vous un effort généreux.
Sur Titus et sur moi réglez votre conduite.
Je l'aime, je le fuis; Titus m'aime, il me quitte.
Portez loin de mes yeux vos soupirs et vos fers.
Adieu: servons tous trois d'exemple à l'univers
De l'amour la plus tendre et la plus malheureuse
Dont il puisse garder l'histoire douloureuse.
Tout est prêt. On m'attend. Ne suivez point mes pas.
                    (A Titus)
Pour la derniére foix, adieu, Seigneur.
ANTIOCHUS
Hélas!
                                                                (V,7)

Prince, after this farewell, you yourself may judge
That I do not consent to leave that which I love
To go far from Rome and listen to other vows.
Live, and make an effort that is generous.
Govern your conduct by Titus and by me.
I love and flee him, Titus loves and abandons me.
Take far from my eyes your sighs and your chains.
Farewell: let all three of us serve the universe
As an example of the tenderest, most unhappy love,
Of which it could preserve the sorrowful story.
All is ready. They await me. Do not follow me.
                    (To Titus)
For the last time lord, farewell.
ANTIOCHUS
   Alas!

Here, in these last words of the play, Roman duty has not conquered love.[3] Love perdures in a tragic acceptance of loss. The sense of love, as Titus says, here invests only himself, a person who would cease to be himself if he abandoned the empire and ran away to some corner of it with his beloved — the project he has silently been resisting and finally voices under the full pressure of her collapse before the first stresses of parting.

Racine's people transcend those stresses. The transcendence embodies itself equally in participants whose differences in sex and amorous status give different intermediate postures to noble lovers who are identical in their final stance. What has been exacted from these lovers is a demonstration of the profound nobility that made them in the first place capable of the love they must renounce. That capability is the normal condition in Racine's plays, as in Corneille's, though a bad Narcisse, a good Burrhus, or a merely political Acomat may fall short of it.

On this stage, evocation is purification. The events, rather than destroying the person necessarily (both Phèdre and Hippolyte do die; and Corneille's Polyeucte is martyred), force out into the open the pure essence of his nobility. The human is shown in terms of its transcendental, and necessary, capacity for renunciation. Andromaque shames Hermione and Oreste, and lives; while life is a small boon to the Néron who has killed Brittanicus.

In the exempla of this theatre, the effort of producing coherence from complexity has been forced to the point where the complexity itself disappears. It disappears in the play's heartfelt call to transcendence-in-loss, the only possible consistency. Racine bends Euripides towards the simplicity of this exalted consistency. The audience, sitting squarely silent before the enactment, has to be celebrating this exaltation if it is also responding.

Chapter One

DISPLACEMENT AND CONDENSATION
IN *BRITANNICUS*

1

In Racine's theatre, as in Corneille's, all the means of poetic language are made uniform. The dramatic tempo holds to an evenness of pace for which the Aristotelian unities stand as convenient touchstones of external definition.[4] The recitative language, the intensified action, are brought to bear on the creation of a restrained idealism, felt at the outset of a play to dominate this staged world. Ideals are not discovered so much as measured, and measured evenly, in a total world of unified presentation. But under the pressure created by the very act of unification there appears an ambivalent shift; the condensation of effect creates a displacement.

Their faces open to the spectators, and not masked, standing generally above the spectators rather than below, the players of the *Grand Siècle* act at the margin of tensions that the poetry of Racine brings to a perilous unity. Their sex, too, is as plain as their faces, where the Jacobean theatre had still been no more "liberated" than the Greek in having men act women's parts. This openness, threatened outside the theatre by the law that kept celebrated actors from being buried in hallowed ground, does not itself find a spatial equivalent on this stage. It does not seek the panoramic openness of the Elizabethans or even the open air of the Greeks. Rather it contains ambivalences by exhibiting the fixity into which the society itself, by its customs, keeps them bound: the "unity of place" is observed, and on a scene mostly indoors; if Phèdre is brought outdoors, it is only so that she may expire. But *Britannicus*, like others, runs its course in the labyrinth of a Roman palace.

Even in religious terms, the condemnation of the actor was ambivalent; Louis XIV stood as godfather for a child of Molière.[5] The ambivalence, the shadiness, of the theatre, finds in its social circumstances not only more severe laws than the English ones, but a far more formidable opponent than the Puritan Gosson. Nicole, himself, the master of Port-Royal—a monastery whose extreme idealism existed ambivalently under the shadow of suspected heresy—speaks of the *poète du théâtre* as an *empoisonneur public*. The orphan Racine had been educated at Port-Royal, and that background charges not only his sense of uneasiness about his vocation, or about any worldliness whatever; it puts him doubly at the margin of the faith, because Port-Royal was challenged by the church as much as it challenged the mundane world. Jansenism was as suspect as the theatre. The climate of devoted band amid the uneasy enthralled is only secularized when Racine moves from Jansenism to the theatre.

Racine was stung enough by Nicole's remark, made in passing against another writer, to have replied twice. And Goldmann, pointing out that this episode comes precisely between the last apprentice tragedy, *Alexandre*, and the first "great" one, *Andromaque*, insists that his "besoin de pureté" exacerbated by the conflict, brought him to make the leap.[6] Duvignaud[7] and Mauron,[8] on the other hand, are willing to attribute his sudden mastery of passion to the professional vivification of his love affair with Du Parc, which happened at the same key moment.

The tension is there, wherever we look, in the life of the poet as well as in the society around him. The play succeeds in unifying this tension into idealism through mechanisms familiar to us from Freud's study of dreams, though more gloriously than in dreams, and more triumphantly in the linguistic synthesis of dramatic enactment. It operates, briefly, by "displacement," and also by "condensation."

To take a long look at displacement first, and in a single play, it would be a mistake to assume that the Romanism of *Britannicus* signifies only what it includes, the Renaissance exemplum of an ideal secular empire. It also displaces what it excludes, the Christian world which permeates not only the allegiances but also the sensibilities of the "inner" audience for whom Racine is writing.[9] Classical Rome allows the Christian writer to rebuild his Christian gestures from scratch, or to contemplate sacred impulses by setting them on the *tabula rasa* of an ideal secular world; so the thrust of Corneille's Romanism operates in *Polyeucte*. In *Britannicus* the end of the play alone expands the suggested analogy, as does the end alone of *Iphigénie*. Junie's last act is to make religiosity explicit, though it is still displaced into the pagan religion, of course: she joins the Vestal Virgins. To call her psychology here an easy anachronism would be to ignore the careful consideration of Tacitus that Racine undertook in preparing for the play; he had to force the material to impose a Christian displacement upon it. Junie's act offers a willed convergence of a Roman convention with the kind of sensibility which would retire to a monastery, one defined not in the positive terms of a normal cloister, but in the negative terms of total withdrawal from the world, terms very much like those formulated by the "extremist" party at Port-Royal. Racine's own Port-Royal in this resembled his notion of the Vestal Virgins more than it did, say, the Saint-Cyr of Madame de Maintenon, for which he later wrote *Esther* and *Athalie*.

Port-Royal differs from the royal Saint-Cyr, and resembles the Vestals, in another more specific sense: the Vestals were absolutely isolated from the emperor, the one place in the empire beyond Nero's reach. So Junie discovers within herself offstage as she runs off at the news of Britannicus' death and keeps running, while Narcisse, who tries to catch her, is torn to pieces by the crowd. Similarly, Port-Royal, for being out of favor with the court of the *Roi Soleil*, was fortified in its isolation from the court it condemned.

Racine, moreover, insists on his historicity, to the point of bringing up in his preface to the play what he says none of his critics had noticed, the fact he documents from Aulus Gellius, that Junie would have been too old to be admitted to the Vestals. In response he confects a casuistic argument, unconvincing for us but obviously necessary for him (and so for the play), that in extreme cases the age limit would be waived. The convergence of his idealized secular world with an ideal (and so Christian) one involves, then, not the free creativity that allows anachronism, but a willed historicity that puts a deliberate strain on the convergence.

Rome itself was not easy for him: *Britannicus* is his first Roman play, and also his last. (The later *Bérénice* takes place at Rome, but two of its three principals are from the East.) It was not easy for Shakespeare either, who had, so to speak, to get all the way through eight history plays before *Julius Caesar* became possible; the barbarism of *Titus Andronicus* being simpler imaginatively as well as past the Ideal Empire in time. But Shakespeare's stage is more elastic, though the mechanisms of resource to the classical world exhibit, for him too, a negative, non-Christian signification as well as the positive "mirror of princes." Racine had directly before him the plays of Corneille on Roman subjects: *Horace, Cinna, Polyeucte, Pompey*, and others, and still he did not take recourse to the charged Roman ground. When he finally did come round to Rome, after the distraction and blockage of a comedy about lawyers, Corneille sat in the first-night audience and was not pleased.

The displacement onto Rome allows the audience to entertain only the possibility of convergence with its own ideals: left ambiguous (and not simply concealed by distance) is the question of whether the intrigues of a pagan court really resembled those of a Christian. In the world of secular government, the absolute authority to which the *Roi Soleil* aspired is immunized by locating the ruler of it at Rome, "Néron," someone who lacks Christianity not only technically but in any of the natural senses that could be attributed to Burrhus, Britannicus, or Junie. The name "Néron" alone, as Racine says in his preface, "fasait entendre quelque chose de plus que cruel." Even the secular authority is displaced into a viciousness unnatural and unchristian, and the extremity of the "monstre naissant" leaves open its angle of displacement from the mean of an ideal secular Rome. Here, however, Néron is imprisoned as much by his willfulness as Titus later is by his perceptive generosity in *Bérénice*.

Displaced onto the past, Racine's world strains toward the sense of a common psychic determination in the erotic sphere, finally, rather than the religious. Still, the three spheres— governmental, erotic, and religious—exhibit their strains in a displaced ground of space, time, and altered signification, as well as in the specific "dramatic" tensions among the personages. "Rome" taken just as a word carries some faint tinge of what it has been displaced from, the center of a religious authority for which that monosyllable stands in the theological present of the audience's real world. When Junie says "O Ciel, sauvez Britannicus," the capitalization in the text of the word "Ciel" insists on the strain towards convergence, as the same word does for Phèdre (I,4) in her first response both to Thésée's death and to the fact that it comes just as she has revealed her guilty love. Butor conjectures that a hidden analogy to the Christian sacrifice has led Racine to state, as he does, that without the figure of Eriphile, substituted as a sacrifice for Iphigénie at the last moment, he would not have dared to write that play.[10]

Leaving aside Shakespeare's tremendous uses, classical figures in the Renaissance are normally employed either for simple artifice, or simple example, or both. When Ronsard speaks of *Vénus*, when Racine himself in his poems speaks of a Nymph and *les Graces* and *Dieux*, they mean to say some-

thing like this; "in choosing through the artifice of my poem
terms from a mythology which we regard as largely imaginary,
I have pointed up an imaginary and artifice-like quality in the
love, as well as a simplicity not unlike that of the ancient world
whose own simplicity my act of displacement may be taken to
throw into relief." Now in Racine's plays all this strategy is
gone—is in fact, as it were, itself displaced into a convergence
of earnestness desperately dramatized, in the *Diane* of *Iphigénie*, the *dieux* of *Britannicus* and others, and markedly in
the *Vénus* of *Phèdre*. In that final secular play, Racine maxi-
mizes the strain towards convergence, and the *Vénus tout
entière à sa proie attachée*, takes the artifice-displacement of
Ronsard and throws it onto the stage as a desperate struggle-
unto-the-death against something like the principalities and
powers of a Christian other world. The secular world recreates
the Christian sentiment of remorse too, and it is not just the
dying Phèdre who is to feel remorse. Agrippine prophesies that
Néron will be tortured by it after he kills Junie.

To call this *dieu* either baldly classical or even absent over-
simplifies it. The dramatic displacement of Racine does not
equal the theology of Port-Royal, whose *dieu* Goldmann
convincingly calls *caché*. In the plays, a sense of ultimate
rightness is worked through the feelings of the spectators, who
are brought up not to the hidden God, but rather to a resolution
that ultimately identifies the common impulse in any human
expression: to emphasize not the difference of what has been
displaced, but the analogy, as between secular Rome and
Christian France. So, in effect, Racine claims in the preface to
Iphigénie when he says "mes spectateurs ont été émus des
mêmes choses qui ont mis autrefois en larmes le plus savant
peuple de la Grèce."

All the displacements work toward an emotion, as always in
drama. Seen in terms of his plotted complexity, Racine displaces
his subject, and bars his personages too, from one another, as
well as displacing his ideological given. If Oreste loves Hermione,
then Hermione loves Pyrrhus; and if Pyrrhus loves Andromaque,

she is blocked by duty to her dead husband. If Junie and Britannicus love each other, the very trust that has led them to this sentiment gets subverted by the duplicity of Néron, whose love is no less, though differently, blocked. If Titus loves a loving Bérénice and is also emperor—the maximum condition, so to speak—then his duty keeps him from marrying someone whom his subjects could not countenance. These difficulties are not factitious, of course, but real and present during Racine's lifetime. Louis XIV wept when he was told that he could not marry Marie Mancini, and years later he refused to see her when she came with her husband to be received at court.

2

There is, along with so strenuous a displacement, a constant condensation of effect. Again in the preface to *Iphigénie*, Racine goes on to cite Aristotle, rendering his tragic effects of *eleos* and *phobos* (Racine knew Greek well) intensively as *la compassion et la terreur*, terms he repeats in the preface to *Phèdre*.

Seen in terms of the unified world into which these love-displaced characters are drawn, the three spheres of government, love, and religion are condensed, as well as displaced on stage; they become sources for displaying not only the *compassion* for and *terreur* in human limitation, but the majesty of transcending it. For, to begin with, the displacement into a non-Christian world has the effect of reducing the three spheres to two: government and love occupy the stage, and religion stands only as an ultimate recourse, as it never could in a play exacting some sense that the king rules by divine right, or that the salvation of the infinite soul lying behind the beloved person outweighs all one's devotion.

The spheres of government and love are kept discrete to test the characters' ideals; a ruler is never allowed to be a happy lover in Racine, or a lover to be a happy ruler. At the same time the ideal of each sphere is an absolute. Each ideal is in that sense invested with an implicit emotional justification for which, as Barthes points out, the word "foi" does duty in both the erotic and the governmental spheres.[11] The absolute values are no less absolute for exhibiting the possibility of a tragic conflict.

It is the absoluteness of the situation in which someone is caught that evokes our *compassion*; it is the limitation that evokes our *terreur*: Néron himself, at the end, no less than Phèdre, is magnificently the object of both feelings. The possible good emperor, who in the words of a not-too-tender mother "commence... par où finit Auguste," has become the actual bad emperor, separated forever from Junie in his love. And in his divorce from the honor in government, Néron will always be tormented by the conscience for which a plainspeaking soldier we see is made to stand and not the skillful moral philosopher who is kept offstage—Burrhus and not Seneca. In the words of that mother's final speech, "tes remords te suivront comme autant de furies."

The two final images of Néron in the play, the governmental one and the erotic one, condense him and condense those spheres, as they condense the mere *terreur* of his governmental role into the *terreur* and *compassion* of his erotic frustrations. The first image is given in the words of Burrhus, sadder over the transmogrification of his pupil than he has been over the death of Britannicus. Not only does Néron, in the prior scene, pretend glacially to his mother that he has nothing to do with the poisoning of his half-brother, but, as Burrhus says to his mother and to us:

Mais s'il vous faut, Madame, expliquer ma douleur,
Néron l'a vu mourir sans changer de couleur.

(V,7)

But, lady, if I must explain to you my sorrow,
Nero, as he saw him die, did not change color.

This picture in our terrifed eyes breaks its glacial calm in the next and final view of the emperor, which mixes compassion with terror when the strength of Junie's withdrawal is measured by the extremity of the horrible composure it has destroyed (Néron is described after the death of Narcisse):

> *Il rentre. Chacun fuit son silence farouche.*
> *Le seul nom de Junie échappe de sa bouche.*
> *Il marche sans dessein; ses yeux mal assurés*
> *N'osent lever au ciel leurs regards égarés.*

(V,8)

> He returns. Everyone flees his savage silence.
> All that comes out of his mouth is Junie's name.
> He paces aimlessly; his ill-assured eyes
> Do not dare raise their lost looks to the sky.

In this world, government and love demonstrably concentrate into a unified ideal whose *honneur* Nero has traduced at his inner peril. Love expands a mind that governs, so that it at least entertains the possibility of good government; and in that sense love implies government here, if not the other way around. Titus' very sensibility to love makes him the good governor who decides to renounce his love. Agrippine and Narcisse, in their immunity to passion, are likewise unable to grasp the higher ideal of ruling, even as they steer Néron into it or away from it for their own ends; while Néron's susceptibility to love, like Pyrrhus' in *Andromaque*, puts him on that true plane where ability to rule could operate in some kind of harmony with the gods. Of course the *monstre* is always *naissant* in Néron, and his love for Junie is kindled in an atmosphere somewhat heated with sadism. This still does not allow us to postulate, with Barthes, two kinds of love in Racine; it is not clear, for example, that such "bad" lovers as Atalide in *Bajazet*, Eriphile in *Iphigénie*, Pyrrhus and Hermione in *Andromaque*, or even wholly Néron himself, are succumbing to a *coup de foudre* and not to a gradually awakening feeling; or that their passion has primary attributes that differ other than in nuances of tone from that of ideal characters.

Once awakened, however awakened, the feeling of love is absolute. The absoluteness is exhibited to the audience, and concentrated in interaction, tragically, with another absolute, that of instituted rule. In so far as both are absolutes, their condensation serves as an analogy to that other absolute which encompasses them, the Almighty who himself at once governs and loves, as his creatures, in this view, cannot. Their very incapacity serves, in fact, to suggest their distance from something that in the world of Racine cannot be other than Himself, present in his absences, to adapt a maxim Goldmann cites from Saint-Cyr.[12] A play, inevitably swayed by love, is inevitably decided by some combination of love and government. Britannicus, in his death, serves to measure Néron, the central character here. That death seals Néron in his monstrosity and renders totally ironic the last words of Burrhus and of the play, *"Plût aux Dieux que ce fût le dernier de ses crimes!"*

The condensation of absolutes to the degree that they tragically block one another goes, in one way, beyond the world of Corneille, where the supersession of family honor by love in Chimène amounts to a reconciliation of the two goals. All ideals are sacrificed to Rome in *Horace* and in *Cinna* as well. In *Polyeucte* an amorous rivalry compounded with a rivalry between Christ and Empire is still not too great for a reconciliation by conversion all round: Christianity intrudes and transcends, directly.

But the terms are the same; Racine has wrought their condensation more economically. He has done the same, too, with the conditions of space and time in his plays. It would be a mistake to regard the concern for the unities in these writers as a merely antiquarian or even merely formalistic interest. The adapted injunctions of Aristotle offer a ready vehicle for condensing events under conditions where condensation comes to seem purity.

In fact, such a condensation on stage does implicitly postulate purity, in so far as a heightening of the initial conditions on stage suggests it, and gives a degree of abstractness, if not of absoluteness, to what is happening as these plays conceive it, to action.

They offer, of course, that third essential unity too. But before looking at the unity of action in them, we should notice two other ways that these plays condense their representations.

One is the diction of the speeches. This verse, remarkably, offers very little of the apocalyptic chiaroscuro of Shakespeare, or even of Sophocles. Instead, the hard even light of its terms produces steadily a peerless version of what elsewhere I have called the refined style, a measured and somewhat abstract series of terms more noteworthy for high evenness than for special beauties.[13] One may translate its most noted sonorities back into fairly simple, intradramatic signification. For instance, "La fille de Minos et de Pasiphaé" puts the two parents of Phèdre on either half of a caesura. She is the daughter of a king, but equally the daughter of a woman notable for a monstrous and illicit passion. She is the daughter of a king known to be a judge in the underworld, and the Minos in her is all the while judging herself—it later fears to meet him in the underworld (IV,6)—while the royal princess in her is letting her have her own way to give the Pasiphae in her its head. All this gets ominous strength from being put in the mouth of Hippolyte as the very first mention of Phèdre in the play. To take another example,

"*Dans l'Orient désert quel devint mon ennui*",

In the desert East what did my boredom become.

there is at least one oxymoron here (*orient* with *désert*) and probably two (*ennui* is the state of being which knows no becoming, no *devenir*). All the terms, in any case, ironically sketch in a situation which *devint* more *désert*, more full of *ennui* than ever, once the *Orient* of the play's conclusion receives back the separate Antiochus and Bérénice. They will have become richer by their divided presence, and still more tragic than Antiochus was while there in the solitude he here describes.

Equally abstract, equally complex in their potential condensation (rather than Shakespearean expansion) are such lines as Junie's to Britannicus:

> *Combien tout ce qu'on dit est loin de ce qu'on pense!*
> *Que la bouche et le coeur sont peu d'intelligence!*
>
> (V,1)

How far is all they say from what they think!
How little do mouth and heart understand one another!

Of this striking division we are to see an even more striking example at the imminent conclusion of the play: the *combien* seems a plenum at the moment, but *combien* will become even greater when Néron has done his last deed, finding his *bouche* able to utter the single word "Junie," so that the union of his intelligence with his *coeur* at last will be only terrible: he will never allow himself a single, wholly honorable *pensée*.

But any lines will do. Each line is condensed onto the high plane of this measured abstractness. Words like *orgueil* and *courage, amour* and *empire*, the *fléchir* and *affranchir* especially noted by Mauron,[14] *implorer* and *expirer, chercher* and *cacher*, operate on the plane of their many abstract fellows. As Lapp says, "In the Racinian tragic drama, certain words develop through three stages, none of them chronologically or mutually exclusive: (1) words, which through the influence of preciosity have lost their metaphorical or metonymical quality, function primarily as euphemisms; (2) they become 'demetaphorized', so that they function concretely; (3) they are 'remetaphorized', and they either rediscover an earlier metaphorical meaning, or assume new metaphorical or symbolical force."[15] Lapp has in view such words as *yeux* and *sang*. One may amplify such a potential list with the abstractions or semiabstractions discussed above, with certain verbs, and even at times adjectives and adverbs, to the point where this intensification-condensation may be felt as the salient and even-toned determinant of Racine's style.

The second instrument of condensation is the progression of the lines. Each pair of them is a little plenum, closed off by the rhymes, whose own sets of order offer a repertoire of logical identification and contrast, a gratuitous "marking," to use a linguistic term, which must carry such a logical charge not to be wholly frivolous. Across the stage barrier, the rhythm in the mouths of actors announces the overdetermination, the special condensation of expression, which carries an over-determination of their extreme situation, and may be taken to correspond to that overdetermination of effects that Lacan follows Freud in characterizing as the special feature of the unconscious.

Thus the condensation of the rhymes, in so far as they are functional—or, so to speak, overfunctional—performs the same kind of connection between instance and pattern which, in another social circumstance (the Greek) is given by myth, or by mythlike beings (the "tragic" heroes of Shakepeare). Overdetermined by the linguistic marking of rhyme, and unified by the even movement of the rhythms, the Racinian couplet provides the first term for the perpetuating evenness of its condensation, by operating as a base unit of dramatic speech just twice as large as a given line. The given line itself, in turn, the caesura-split alexandrine, has just twice the number of syl-lables of its ruled hexasyllabic half.

The language itself, again, is one of multiple coordinated signs that draw each other taut and commandeer ever new aspects of "the same" situation, the implicit plenum. In *Britannicus*, every conjunction for the terms in the play—*Rome, empire, maîtresse, ce qu'on veut, mère, fils, frère, souhaiter,* and the proper names themselves—is loaded fully and propels its load evenly forward. The very grammatical complication of Junie's summary to Britannicus puts in one line of involved tenses what could be spelled out as an equivalent to the labyrinth of time in which they find themselves:

> *Enfin, j'aurais voulu n'avoir jamais aimé.*
>
> (III,7)

> At last, I would have wished to have never loved.

So uniformly like a plenum are these speeches, that they can only momentarily vary their pace. One line may do a full job and still not seem stichomathic. There is no room for a chorus, rhythmically, though for other reasons a chorus would be an intrusion—not because the audience has no surrogates here, which is Goldmann's reason.[16] These characters exist in condensed relation, not in the isolation he urges, and they are all surrogates for the noble audience which recognizes even in pagan Rome a Christian Versailles, whereas the Athenians who attended the theatre of Dionysus could not have visualized their city as being mainly on the wrong side of the Trojan war.

The rhythms seem so condensed that any couplet, or any number of couplets, will amplify but not add to the situation. On the other hand, at this even pace, the intrusion into this plenum of a surprise that alters the conditions and reasserts the unity takes place again and again, sometimes in a single line:

> *Narcisse, c'en est fait, Néron est amoureux,*

says the emperor (II,1), changing at one stroke the calculations of that totally prudent and utterly wrong underling. And the plenum of his interview with Junie breaks from one ironic set into another when she asks who the husband is to be whom he will bestow on her:

> *Et quel est donc, Seigneur, cet époux?*
> *Moi, Madame.*
>
> (II,3)

> And who is then this husband, lord?
> Lady, it is I.

His two words, for all their succinctness, cannot seem more condensed, or more expansive, than the long speech which follows, so even are the rhythms, so totally does the abstractness of one couplet, or a speech which is merely a fragment of one, encompass the situation. "Moi, Madame" is neither fast nor slow: its *coup de grace* sinks inexorably into Junie, and into us.

So Narcisse's

> *Ah, Dieux! A L'Empereur portons cette nouvelle.*
>
> (III,6)

> Gods! Let us carry this news to the emperor.

when Britannicus meets Junie without the sadistic surveillance, and his duplicity breaks clearly forth.

So Néron's answer to Burrhus,

> *Ma gloire, mon amour, ma sûreté, ma vie,*
>
> (IV,3)

> My glory, my love, my security, my life.

seemingly total, is rendered provisional by its rhyme ("envie") as well as by Burrhus's answer, "Non,"—and also, as always, by the series of events. So Néron's ominous single-line speech before the poisoning:

Viens, Narcisse. Allons voir ce que nous devons faire.
                                                        (IV,4)

Come, Narcisse. Let us see what we must do.

The antithesis of "voir" and "faire," the ironic evocation of duty (he may still, after all, just possibly be heeding Burrhus's injunctions), and the summoning of Narcisse, directly offer a timed plenum of equivalence to any other point of the action, with suitable adjustment.

3

The adjustment is on the part of the audience: and it is an ironic adjustment: one imports dramatic irony, which is laid dynamically through the series of events at every point, rather than given as a full-scale platform from which the audience views the action; as in a Greek play, where the audience, foreknowing the myth's whole series of events, measures the events on stage by the distance (dramatic irony) of what it knows. The name Néron is ominous, and the ominousness keeps the stage irony dynamically present. But the name does not evoke any specific series of events, as do the names Andromaque, Iphigénie, or even Phèdre; there is no platform of foreknowledge from which the audience can distance its responses.

The irony does function by quick strokes from scene to scene, as sometimes in the tragedy of the Greeks, whom Racine always has somewhat in view. But it remains, dynamically, something expected in an uncertain way, as never quite in Greek tragedy, where it is uniformly present. In Racine, we compassionately wait to be terrified by the alteration of the plenum, by the incursion of a person from without or a conversion from within that will set the world once more tragically into its heartbreaking limits, condensing when it might have expanded.

This action is unified through the condensation into a minimum number of characters, who have a minimum number of encounters. Each of the encounters has the aspect of a *scène à faire*, and inobvious ones or merely illustrative ones are rigorously excluded, even the seemingly necessary encounter between Narcisse and Burrhus that Louis Racine quotes and Racine himself edited out.[17] Condensation is achieved in the Tacitean complexity of a political situation here not reduced: many more characters are named than appear, and the condensed love-rupture intrudes on a closed world where every alliance has a long, manifold emotional and political history.[18]

Moreover, as Goldmann insists,[19] though rather differently than he interprets, the large "moment" of the play offers a series of moments, each one of which is a kind of plenum, unifying the action—from the very beginning, where the exclusion of Agrippine would seem to mark the entire world of Néron, on to the very end, where his solitude would seem to enclose him wholly in the self Burrhus hopes will not (but we know will) become wholly actualized. Every scene is, in Goldmann's emphasis, *pour la dernière fois.*[20] The incursion of a new person always introduces not just a new auditor, or even a new factor, but a shifting of the "balance" to which Agrippine at one moment explicitly refers:

Il faut qu'entre eux et lui je tienne la balance,
Afin que quelque jour, par une même loi,
Britannicus la tienne entre mon fils et moi.

(I,1)

It must be that between them and him I hold the scale,
So that some day, by a selfsame law,
Britannicus may hold it between my son and me.

Consequently, more significant than the traditional five-act division is the French convention of numbering a new scene with every entrance or exit: each single scene does, in fact, change the given plenum in a way that tends toward surprise (and consequently, by virtue of the other condensations, to comment ironically on what has gone ahead). Burrhus, intruding on Agrippine (I,2), offers a justification for Néron which at first makes him look bad and her good (though in the irony of an evolving plenum the reverse is the case). In the next scene (3), Agrippine and Narcisse "help" Britannicus to go to her minion Pallas for help. Narcisse, in the next, counsels a discretion, which, in the light of his subsequently revealed badness, must be taken as interested advice. And in the next scene, before Britannicus can get to him, we learn that Pallas has been banished. The next scene introduces into this deadlock the ironic surprise that the political prisoner Junie is an object of love, a fact that gives Narcisse new leverage, in a new plenum, to urge Néron to assert his centrality in the plenum: to divorce his wife and betray Britannicus. This leads Néron to reveal a new dimension of his character: he mounts the sadistic scene we are shortly to inspect—his interview with Junie. Her subsequent scene with the emperor brings him, in a rapid series, to the irritation that justifies the menace by which Narcisse concludes the second act: "perdons les misérables," a phrase which will ironically reveal its full truth when at the play's end the speaker himself is killed, though again we have, in this point as in all, a plenum where the dynamic might well come to a standstill.

But to posit the real possibility of a standstill would be to reckon without the absoluteness of demand in rule and possession in love, which keeps the plenum changing to another. Human inadequacy in this enacted universe exhibits itself as being such that no plenum does not exhibit limits which at once challenge and evoke the demonstration of love in honor or honor in love.

Burrhus at this point is a new element just because he is unchanged vis-à-vis the now altered Néron. He is able to recall his emperor into a capitulation he alerts us about by revealing (III,2) that he cannot quite believe it. Indeed, reckoning on Néron alone, he is reckoning without the dynamic of his inter-action with Agrippine, who enters and reveals a fairly desperate plan Burrhus manages to check, though Agrippine continues in her rage (III,4) after he leaves. In the next scene, Narcisse checks Britannicus' growing enthusiasm at growing allegiances by insinuating insistently that Junie's affections as well as her person will have succumbed to Néron's mere power. Junie herself breaks this impossible plenum by her very arrival, and by summarizing a situation that, though it has ultimately to do with his life, Britannicus misunderstands. His delay brings about his arrest in the next scene.

The entrance of Burrhus, again, would seem to check Néron, but instead the emperor checks his tutor. Now, for the first time since Act 1, Scene 1, we are given at the beginning of Act 4 a second council between Burrhus and Agrippine: but what has intervened between their meetings carries with it the forces that will disrupt their seemingly total understanding. Indeed, Agrippine alters the next scene, the first and only interview in the play between son and mother, calling Néron an *ingrat*, a phrase which leads the ambivalent son of this virago to agree to pardon Britannicus, fraudulently. In the next scene (IV, 4), Burrhus seemingly overdetermines this plenum by adding his voice to Agrippine's and finally carrying the day. But the next scene reverses all this by turning the advocacy over to Narcisse. After appeals to rumor and to Néron's love for Junie, the evil counsellor finally wins him over by asserting that Agrippine has been bragging about her ascendancy.

Néron now has the poison on the one hand but his virtue on the other, and we do not know for certain—though his exit at the end of Act 4, Scene 4, is most ominous—that he will tip the balance in the successive ironies of Act 5, until we are given the news of Britannicus's death.

The irony, at any given point, remains, like the condensed language, a means for further condensing an already condensed situation, or for further displacing an already displaced one.

And it is total: we know at many points little more than anyone except the victims. There is no Shakespearian and Jacobean manipulation of dramatic ironies. Junie and Britannicus are sorrowful enough in their separation, in their sufferings since childhood, without his having to die. They are kept enough apart by the mere treacherous presence of Narcisse, ironically unknown to them (he is still "cher Narcisse" even to the watchful Junie), without having the emperor concealed and Junie a terrified puppet. Néron forces her to tell Britannicus to leave without revealing her love in order not to lose him, in the famous scene that we may dwell on somewhat:

BRITANNICUS
Madame, quel bonheur me rapproche de vous?
Quoi? Je puis donc jouir d'un entretien si doux?
Mais parmi ce plaisir quel chagrin me dévore!
Hélas! puis-je espérer de vous revoir encore?
Faut-il que je dérobe, avec mille détours,
Un bonheur que vos yeux m'accordaient tous les jours?
Quelle nuit! Quel réveil! Vos pleurs, votre présence
N'ont point de ces cruels désarmé l'insolence?
Que faisait votre amant? Quel démon envieux
M'a refusé l'honneur de mourir à vos yeux?
Hélas! dans la frayeur dont vous étiez atteinte,
M'avez-vous en secret adressé quelque plainte?
Ma Princesse, avez-vous daigné me souhaiter?
Songiez-vous aux douleurs que vous m'alliez coûter?
Vous ne me dites rien? Quel accueil! Quelle glace!
Est-ce ainsi que vos yeux consolent ma disgrâce?
Parlez. Nous sommes seuls: notre ennemi trompé,
Tandis que je vous parle, est ailleurs occupé.
Ménageons les moments de cette heureuse absence.
JUNIE
Vous êtes en des lieux tout pleins de sa puissance.
Ces murs mêmes, seigneur, peuvent avoir des yeux;

Et jamais l'Empereur n'est absent de ces lieux.
BRITANNICUS
Et depuis quand, madame, êtes-vous si craintive?
Quoi? Déjà votre amour souffre qu'on le captive?
Qu'est devenu ce coeur qui me jurait toujours
De faire à Néron même envier nos amours?
Mais bannissez, madame, une inutile crainte.
La foi dans tous les coeurs n'est pas encore éteinte;
Chacun semble des yeux approuver mon courroux;
La mère de Néron se déclare pour nous.
Rome, de sa conduite elle-même offensée...
JUNIE
Ah! seigneur, vous parlez contre votre pensée.
Vous-même, vous m'avez avoué mille fois
Que Rome le louait d'une commune voix;
Toujours à sa vertu vous rendiez quelque hommage.
Sans doute la douleur vous dicte ce langage.
BRITANNICUS
Ce discours me surprend, il le faut avouer.
Je ne vous cherchais pas pour l'entendre louer.
Quoi? Pour vous confier la douleur qui m'accable,
A peine je dérobe un moment favorable,
Et ce moment si cher, madame, est consumé
A louer l'ennemi dont je suis opprimé?
Qui vous rend à vous même, en un jour, si contraire?
Quoi? Même vos regards ont appris à se taire?
Que vois-je? Vous craignez de rencontrer mes yeux?
Néron vous plairait-il? Vous serais-je odieux?
Ah! si je le croyais... Au nom des Dieux, Madame,
Éclaircissez le trouble où vous jetez mon âme.
Parlez. Ne suis-je plus dans votre souvenir?
JUNIE
Retirez-vous, Seigneur, l'Empereur va venir.
BRITANNICUS
Après ce coup. Narcisse, à qui dois-je m'attendre? (II,6)

SC. VII—Entre Néron.

NÉRON

Madame...

JUNIE

Non, seigneur, je ne puis rien entendre.
Vous, êtes obéi. Laissez couler du moins
Des larmes dont ses yeux ne seront pas témoins.

BRITANNICUS

Lady, what happiness brings me close to you?
What, I may then enjoy a converse so tender?
But in this pleasure what sadness devours me!
Alas, may I hope to see you once again?
Must I with a thousand indirections steal
A happiness your eyes gave me every day?
What a night! What a waking! Your tears, your presence
Have not disarmed these cruel men's insolence?
What was your lover doing? What envious demon
Refused me the honor of dying before your eyes?
Alas, in the fright with which you are assailed,
Have you secretly addressed some plaint to me?
My princess, have you deigned to wish for me?
Were you thinking of the sorrows you were to cost me?
You tell me nothing? What a welcome! What ice!
Is this how your eyes console my disgrace?
Speak. We are alone: our deceived enemy
While I speak to you is elsewhere occupied.
Let's profit from the moments of this happy absence.

JUNIE

You are in a place all full of his power.
These walls themselves, my lord, could well have eyes.
And never is the Emperor absent from this place.

BRITANNICUS

And since when, lady, have you been so afraid?
What? Your love already suffers constraint?

What happened to the heart that swore to me always
To make Nero envious of our loves?
But banish, my lady, a useless fear.
Faith is not yet extinguished in all hearts.
Each seems to approve my anger with his eyes.
Nero's mother declares herself for us.
Rome herself, offended by his conduct...

JUNIE

Oh, my lord, you speak against what you think.
You yourself have confessed to me a thousand times
That Rome praised him with a common voice;
You always had some homage to give his virtue.
No doubt sorrow dictates these words to you.

BRITANNICUS

What you say surprises me, I must confess.
I did not seek you out to hear him praised.
What? I would confide the sorrow that crushes me
And can scarcely steal a favorable moment for it.
And, lady, this moment, so dear, is consumed
In praising the enemy by whom I am oppressed?
Who made you in one day so unlike yourself?
What? Even your looks have learned to still themselves?
What do I see? You fear to meet my eyes?
Would Nero please you? I be hateful to you?
Ah, if I thought so! Lady, in the name of the Gods
Enlighten the trouble in which you cast my soul—
Speak. Am I no more in your memory?

JUNIE

Withdraw, my lord, the Emperor is coming.

BRITANNICUS

After this blow, Narcisse, on whom may I wait?
                SC. VII—Enter Nero.

NERO

Lady....

JUNIE

No, my lord, I can hear nothing.

You are obeyed. At least let the tears flow
Of which his eyes will not be witnesses.

The plenum here, for all its sadism, brings us to full *compassion*: the lines, every line, of the "tendre Racine" is drenched with it, and the exemplary situation brings the audience, in the lock-step of these even rhythms, to the very limit of its own absolutes.

Anguish mingles ironically with delight in Néron's injunctions: he himself, too, will have to *renfermer* his *amour* in the *fond* of his *âme*, will have to be more *muet* than this totally restrained Junie could ever be. That plenum is already upon us, but the play mercilessly keeps soliciting our compassion in even lines, keeps implacably awakening our terror. Everyone, not just Néron, is imprisoned in one long *soupir*, except for the present Narcisse, whose blackness is sealed by his very insensitivity to such effects. Britannicus' speech, an abstract stucture, dwells on emotional terms and takes as its terms those emotions the situation demands: *bonheur, doux, plaisir, chagrin, dévore, espérer, bonheur, pleurs, cruels, insolence, envieux, honneur de mourir, frayeur, plainte, souhaiter, douleurs, songiez, glace, consolent, heureuse*. These abstractions are simply named and concatenated. Then again, *craintive, amour, souffre, coeur, amours, envier, crainte, foi, coeurs, courroux, offensée*. And then again, *douleur, accable, cher, craignez, plairait, odieux, trouble, âme, souvenir*. Junie stands forth, for her terrible containment, as more compassionate, not less, because such terms are forbidden to her through the silencing surveillance of the concealed Néron. She cannot so much as mention one of them; she cannot go further than naming the "douleur" by which she describes Britannicus' speech. Otherwise she uses not one word of "love," but instead the words of "government"— *lieux, pleins, puissance, empereur, lieux, Rome, louer, commune voix, sa vertu, hommage*.

It is not just Junie herself who is here forced to express love in the vocabulary of government. All human life, where there are more than two people—and there always are, especially in these plays of tight interrelation—has to be political. The more noble the more political; and all political beings are amorous; the more noble, the more amorous. Others, through rivalry or through power, subvert that possibility of consummation between two people which is the play's focussed ideal. The language and the action, in their displacements and their condensations, confirm the impossibility of an ideal condensation (two totally absorbed lovers) by a necessary displacement (the intrusion of a third party in power or rivalry or both).

The plenum of each play, however, is not subverted by that of each other play. In spite of the thematic distinctions among the plays made by Barthes, Goldmann, Abel, and others, Racine's *tendresse* remains remarkably consistent from play to play. What subverts this plenum is the other possibility in the very ambivalence that the condensations and the displacements are evidencing. It is not that he would change his tune, or that the theatre be rejected for the monastery, which had already been rejected for it; but rather that the theatre be rejected for the world, that first and last of temptations to which Racine would seem to have succumbed when he abruptly dropped the exacerbation of the church-theatre ambivalence to take up another, that of the world. There the church was still, and always, the other half of the ambivalence. The appeal of the church, transferred through the court, will bring him back into the theatre of a still more worldly (and less masterfully ambivalent, and ultimately less religious) kind, the school stage of the pupils of the king's wife's nuns.

Chapter Two

FORCES OF AMBIVALENCE
IN *ATHALIE*

When Racine withdrew from the public theater, there was a long silence. When he broke that silence to produce private theatricals, Eros was withdrawn as a force from the plays. At first it was still a presence: Esther's power over Assuérus derives from the same source as Andromaque's over Pyrrhus or Junie's over Britannicus. But the tension of ambivalence has vanished and with it the dramaturgic lightning, which now is striking elsewhere.

With *Athalie* it will strike in the very sphere that had been foreshortened by condensation and displaced in the public plays, the sphere of religious devotion. The secular tragedies forge a link between *honneur* and *foi* by setting up tensions between two other spheres of human concern, government and love. When religious devotion replaces love in Racine's private plays, the new element does not simply parallel the old: devotion for a Christian must be paramount where love has been all-absorbing. And devotion provides a prior ultimate, where love in Racine's secular tragedies is erected as an ultimate through the action of the play. Moreover, in *Athalie* finally, the sphere of government, which is merely neutral or mysterious as a secular force in *Esther*, becomes fused with religious devotion. The state is a religious state coming into being. It is the throne of David, that locus of both government and devotion, which is being restored.

Still the theatre, as an ambivalent area, was not safe ground
even in a nunnery. When the girls of Saint-Cyr acted the Christian
fable *Polyeucte* in 1688, they still did so during the carnival
time of special license before Lent, and *Athalie* incurred not
only the ambiguous royal disfavor which prevented it from
ever really being produced, but also a religious censure.[21]

In the play the restoration of David's throne through divine
providence is inevitable. Yet, a Catholic theory of free will, and
indeed a theory of that Augustine so popular at Port-Royal,
places exacting burdens on those who would use their free will
to ascertain the will of God, as Joad and Joas and Abner must
do, and as even Athalie does in the process of suffering transformation. Ambivalence still remains, in both predominant
spheres of government and religion, and in the community
between them, an ambivalence that the occasional and private
circumstance of these performances throws into especially
marked relief.

Any theatre, as Duvignaud says,[22] brings always a *dédouble-
ment* or doubling of roles between those on stage and those in
the audience. The stage figures, just by being "out there,"
split the life roles of people in society. The split tends further
to produce a specification of function: we are given certain
types, the clown or the king or the unhappy lover, more often
than certain other types in the society. And the types we get,
as Duvignaud joins many others in emphasizing, are special in
a special way: they tend to fuse elements that in the society at
large are ambivalent, like "clown" or "scapegoat." So, too, on
the audience side of the stage barrier, the audience member has
a special function when in the theatre. He must, for example,
keep quiet. He cannot show his social prerogatives other than
by his seating. In the private theatre at Saint-Cyr, this special
function is odd and explicit: in one dimension the audience are
simply edified girls, seeing an adult play for children; and in
another dimension, they are the overseers of edified girls,
including Madame de Maintenon, the king, and Racine himself,

watching a children's play for adults, over the shoulders of the girls—who themselves, then, become another stage. The girls, too, are the temporary actors, they are the ones who "play" the play.

Duvignaud further offers anomie in the society at large as the motive force for the development of the theatre in this highly ordered world. In this particular play, anomie has been driven firmly elsewhere by the significative structure of the dramatic situation: nothing is less subject to anomie than an edified girl in this audience or a divine boy-king on stage. It has been driven into the condition of the play, where anomie appears, by contrast, in the suppression of unstable ambivalence in each of the spheres, government and religion. Anomie has been suppressed in the fusion of government and religion; whatever is vexed in the lives of these spectators has been triumphantly pacified on stage.

On the one hand, the *Roi Soleil* dominates the world of his royal historian. But on the other hand, ambivalently, Racine leads a life more like that of Jehu and Achab than that of Joas. The king has continued intermittently to persecute the fervent Jansenists who still remain, much as Athalie has persecuted the Jews. Much as certain renegades from Port-Royal, as described in Racine's *Abrégé*, turned on their monastery, does the ex-Israelite Mathan turn on his faith. Ambivalence expresses itself also in Racine's activities at this time; he was writing openly, for public consumption, the official history of the king's campaigns; but writing privately, to be published after his death, *l'Abrégé de l'histoire de Port-Royal.*

The Jews of *Athalie*, in Racine's actual world, are also ambivalent. What the Jansenists are in space the Jews are in time: in the past, God's chosen people; in the present, an unregenerate enclave. The similarity appears emphatically in the likeness of the position of the temple for the kingdom of Athalie to that of Port-Royal for Versailles, as well as in the often noted similarity between the character Joad and the real Grand Arnaud.

There are other similarities between Racine's personal condition and the work, more specific ones, psychoanalytic and thematic. But they take us still further out of the specific play and its context of verbal and presentative signification. Charles Mauron sees in *Athalie*, as in Racine's earlier plays, an opposition between a virago (Athalie, Agrippine, Phèdre, Hermione, etc.) and a tender woman (Josabet, Junie, Aricie, Andromaque, etc.); he sees, too, an isolated child threatened by death (Joas, Iphigénie, Hippolyte, Britannicus, Astyanax).[23] Between these figures, he says, both criminal impulse and superego agree about the nonexistence of the ego. The ego, then, faced with a mother who either abandons or murders, must kill or be killed: Eliacin bears the marks of Athalie's earlier stabbing. Thus the psychoanalytic drive for establishing the ego's survival is deployed onto a providential stage and linked with the divine right of succession to rule over God's chosen people: the ambivalences are made to disappear in the political action of ineffable grace.

Of course to allow finality to Mauron's unconscious connections takes the ambivalences away from the merely private sphere either of Racine's own inner dynamics, so convincingly expounded by Mauron, or the audience's response to the merely psychoanalytic elements in the play. These elements themselves, however, have undergone transformation here. Racine was an orphan but never a prince. The fusions of the figures are at once too complex and too exemplary for us to trace them in an unusually direct way to the psychic life of the author. Athalie herself, indeed, the most pronouncedly borrowed person, contains elements of both Madame de Maintenon and Racine's fostering aunt, Sister Agnès de Saint-Thècle. He himself, in words which recall the speeches of Joas, contrasts these two formidable feminine presences in a letter to Madame de Maintenon that he never sent. Agnès de Saint-Thècle had the force of Athalie in the circumstances of Josabet—except that she lacked a husband. Athalie's husband does not appear on stage, and Madame de Maintenon's, the king himself, stands behind her to guarantee what her patronage of Saint-Cyr also asserts, the benignity of this secretly capricious woman in her declining years. She is served by flattering priests much as Athalie is served by Mathan, and in the very temple of the true God, in a showpiece monastery towards which many of the accusations could be levelled that the voluminous writers of Port-Royal did level generally at the religious life of their time. Saint-Cyr removes the ambivalence from the secular theater, and with it the predatory erotic life, onstage and off. Compounding an adult audience behind the girls restores ambivalence, to which the unreality of the intensely virtuous principals on stage also testifies.

Madame de Maintenon had once been married to a writer, Scarron, whose satires made capital of the ambivalences in the literary life, where Racine had once been subject to that ambivalence in the very act of realizing erotic maturity. Love and the theater divorced him from the religious milieu, itself ambivalent, of his orphan's upbringing. Madame de Maintenon, through erotic activity, had escaped ambivalence, had become pious, and founded Saint-Cyr. She invites Racine to break his poetic silence to celebrate the God who had appeared in muted forms under the tensions of the secular tragedies. After the courtly banter of collaborations on ballet, he does this first in a strictly historical play, which allows Eros some causal role only in a pat situation, *Esther*. And then, in *Athalie*, though he claims to be drawing his plot from Scripture as he had done before, his elaborate summary in the preface is a mere smokescreen concealing his all-but-total invention of this plot. For Bible read psyche: for example, here alone in all of Racine's plays one finds that infantile fantasy so common that Freud gave it a special name, the "family romance" of the child whose visible parents, he believes, hold him in custody as the offspring of real, royal parents. And Racine has intensified this motif by doubling it in a freely invented stroke, by making the aunt and foster mother, Josabet, herself a princess and the sister of a king. The very explicitness here of psyche, rather than history, turns our attention to the special significations. Ambivalence betrays itself in the extravagance of the means taken to iron it out.

For this play, and for *Esther*, the conditions of production were themselves so special that they perhaps qualify as the first chamber plays (differing from masques or other special royal performances again, in being written for a very restricted presentation, for children who are girls in a nunnery school). Its conditions are handled in a way that gives its assertions about providence the ring of desperation. For when *Athalie* was produced, Racine had already begun to fall out of favor with Madame de Maintenon, and where *Esther* had been produced with very elaborate costumes, *Athalie* was done with a simplicity as ominous in the staging as, in the dramatic verse, simplicity is triumphant.

The ambivalences are managed, are surmounted and brought together. Spiritual wisdom and political wisdom are shown to fuse; political vacillation appears in Athalie's changes as itself a spiritual state, in a dramatized action that transcends the vapid piety of Esther. Mathan's political rigor is shown to be only the other face of a spiritual desperation which, if his spirit had been better managed, might have resulted in a faithful priesthood, as he says himself to his confidant Nabal:

> *Né ministre du Dieu qu'en ce temple on adore,*
> *Peut-être que Mathan le servirait encore,*
> *Si l'amour des grandeurs, la soif de commander*
> *Avec Son joug étroit pouvaient s'accommoder.*
>
> (III,3)

> Born minister of the God adored in this temple;
> Nathan would still perhaps be serving him,
> If love of grandeur and thirst to command
> Could be accommodated in his narrow yoke

Political, or military, preoccupation is a narrow yoke too. The principle of interaction between the state's sphere and God's appears nowhere more remarkably than in the interchanges between Abner and Joad. For all his astute experience, his command, and his good will, Abner appears as limited, merely because he does not know the essential fact that will lead him toward the end to do immediate obeisance before Joas.

All persons here, good or bad, perceive in their particular way the manifestation of the divine will as it fuses the kingdom with the temple, the court (to use contemporary terms) with the church: and those two positive values, in the strength of their fusion, spirit away the ambivalences in Versailles, or Port-Royal, or Church, or even Saint-Cyr. Those on the merely political side in *Athalie*, Mathan or Abner, dimly sense the coming fusion. Those wholly for the time on the religious side, the children of Joas and the chorus, also dimly sense it. They serve as passive participants in the active conflict between those whose perceptions have already fused the two spheres: Athalie, who would stifle the religious and so must love its carrier; Joad; Josabet; and at last, revealed for what he is, Joas, who is justified by the simple fact of embodying the religious predominance. So he must win, independently of any justification in the play, which offers none whatever.

The chorus does not react to each separate event, as does the chorus of *Esther*, where fear or hope are transposed at once into a facile emotional register. Here the emotional register responds not to some immediate event, but to a general situation, the one the play dwells on clearly from the very outset and in every encounter. This plenum offers no reversals but merely an intensification focussing on the one central event, Joas' right over Athalie. The chorus, being merely religious, phrases the assumption on which the action proceeds to produce its higher and more unified awareness:

> Ô promesse! ô menace! ô ténébreux mystère!
> Que de maux, que de biens sont prédits tour à tour!
> Comment peut-on avec tant de colère
> Accorder tant d'amour?

                                                              (III,8)

> O promise! O menace! O shadowy mystery!
> What ills, what boons are foretold, each in turn!
> How could so much wrath
> Agree with so much love?

How one can accord so much love with so much wrath is a question this chorus cannot be supposed to answer. The question is a rhetorical question, and it fits not only the girls on stage but the girls in the audience. The real drama goes on through them, and they respond to it. But it also goes on over their heads, and their imagined presence, necessary to the signification of the play, provides, again, the ground of assumption on which the tender Racine allows himself once again to write plays. The condition will be to say what he can in an idiom that cannot offend the ears of young girls. This is not only a negative condition ruling out Eros. It is also a positive condition: the play must exhibit a *piété* and a *morale*, as he says in the preface to *Esther*, though that subject, as he goes on to say, *les frappa d'abord* with being *pleine de grandes leçons d'amour de Dieu*. The lesson for the girls of Saint-Cyr becomes, through them and to the second degree, a literary perception for those, ourselves, imagined as adults present behind this audience; it becomes something *ipso facto* more than a lesson. The simplicity of the play, again, gains its force from the complexity of the ambivalences it has managed, not only between world and God, Church and Jansenists, God and (now godly) theater, but, in the strange and special presentational, and so semantic, conditions of this play, between devout child and self-mastering adult. Racine is himself that adult, who had himself been an orphan boy with a magnificent destiny, raised in the secluded loving care of a vexed monastery, like the child who at last, in this last play, takes over not only the center of the stage but the very conditions governing the dramatic interaction between stage and audience.

The severity of the early tragedies is retained by placing the action in the Hebrew world. This has the advantage of uniting

God and king, combined with the disadvantage of operating before the revelation of the New Testament. Consequently, it can introduce specifically Christian subjects only by overtone— the verse is full of religious *double entendres*—and by typological parallels to such New Testament motifs as the massacre of the innocents, and perhaps also that of Christ in the temple at the age of twelve. These parallels are the more pronounced since the events of the play, again, have been invented rather than found (as he pretends) in the Old Testament.

Furthermore, elements generally kept separate in Racine's actual world are united in the play: the family circle (of the boy Racine, or of the father he became after giving up secular plays), and Port-Royal, and the royal legitimacy, are all elements kept apart in Racine's actual world, if not mutually exclusive. Yet all three are brought together in the unity of place for this play: in the temple where the family of Joad acts to bring the kingdom round to itself, comprising family and religion and royal legitimacy all in one.

This stage, this chamber theatre, is private in two senses: first, because the commissioned performance is done for a particular small group on invitation; and second, because that group is more restricted (girl children) and more devoted to virtue (students at Saint-Cyr) than a normal group. The normal reaction is above and to one side of the audience: it is, as it were, in our heads conjoined with the head of Racine. The effects are muted effects.

They are muted in another way too. Consider how the audience's expectation works, as described by Irving Feldman, who has extrapolated the terms of the Greek myth, known to the audience before the play opens:

> The foreknowledge of the audience is laced with its contradictory hope that it is wrong, and this provides the structural basis for its feeling that the future is unknowable. Therefore: its wish *not* to know (what it fearfully knows *will* take place) throws up to the

audience the daring and unknowableness of all enter-
prise as it enters a world of universal order (equivalent
to the audience's foreknowledge) with which it must
come to terms (equivalent to the audience's coming to
accede to, that is, to will the tragic destiny).

Or, otherwise: the audience feels itself as not knowing
(that is, is "gripped" by the work) in so far as it wishes
to prevent or delay the happening of what it knows
must and will happen. And therefore comes to feel the
audacity of, for example, an Oedipus who is strong
enough to drag the audience into a future from which
it is attempting to drag *him* back.

This is the dialectical basis of the "gripping"—as opposed
to simple suspense or surprise—where the audience's
"not-knowing" is not a state of ignorance but an activity of the audience, its act, to choose a metaphor
from *Oedipus*, of self-blinding.

The "greatness" of a hero like Oedipus consists in his
making the play happen against the wishes of the
audience. *Will*, therefore, must be at the center, for
Oedipus must move the play as a whole against its
greatest enemy: the audience. This struggle is the
drama's comprehensive *agon*.[24]

Now Racine pretends to deliver a known story, but there is
not really a known story of Athalie: he invents it. Moreover,
we do not even have a name with a ring to it, like Néron.
There is such a name, Jezebel, and Jezebel has to be torn to
pieces once again in the dream of Athalie before the prophetic
figure of the unknown temple servant who is to kill her comes
clear in the dream. Athalie is a blank name, and yet the air of
expectation has been conveyed by reference to the Old Testament, and also by the certitude of Joas' bearing, against which
the power of Athalie is shown from the outset to be tottering.

Moreover, what is shown as not at all needing justification is an event as extraordinary as any in the dramatic world—something that complicates Feldman's terms because we both wish it (the throne of David) and are horrified (at the murder of an aged queen). This act of murder by a child combines elements of matricide—so she calls it at the end—with elements of regicide. The Orestes of Aeschylus must mount an extended justification to carry off the former, as must the Brutus of Shakespeare for the latter. And while it is understood that Néron will before long have Agrippine killed, it is also understood that he is a monster, while Joas is a chosen king. So chosen in fact, that he need not shrink before the deed, which is presented, mutedly and expectedly, with neither detail nor much justification: to Joas' question, (IV,1)

Pourquoi ce livre saint, ce glaive, ce bandeau?

Why this holy book, this sword, this band?

the other woman—and not Joad!—replies summarily and evasively:

Tous vos doutes, mon fils, bientôt s'éclairciront.

All your doubts, my son, will soon come clear.

Congruently, he soon comes to declare, as she crowns him, that perhaps he will be a sacrifice (with echoes of *Iphigénie*, as Mauron notes[25]); but his last submissive statement, as easy to reconcile with a psychoanalytic as with a monastic view, implies the power he will assume, since his real father was a king:

Je dois, comme autrefois la fille de Jephté,
Du Seigneur par ma mort apaiser la colère?
Hélas! un fils n'a rien qui ne soit à son père.

(IV,1)

Must I, as long ago Jeptha's daughter did,
Pacify the wrath of the Lord with my death?
Alas, a son has nothing which is not his father's.

The account of the murder is obscured in the messenger Ismael's account of victory:

Nos Lévites...
Ont conté son enfance au glaive dérobé,
Et la fille d'Achab dans le piège tombée.

(V,6)

Our Levites...
Have told of his childhood stolen by the sword
And Ahab's daughter fallen in the snare.

This is all the justification we are given, since Ismael goes on to announce the people's acclaim for a Joas whose act of what we would call assassination has made him triumphant. Athalie, remarkably, is given a final speech longer than the messenger's, longer than any we have had for three scenes. She articulates the awareness of divine providence she has manifested throughout:

Impitoyable Dieu, toi seul as tout conduit.
C'est toi qui me flattant d'une vengeance aisée
M'as vingt fois en un jour à moi-même opposée...
Qu'il règne donc ce fils...
On lui fasse en mon sein enfoncer le couteau.

(V,6)

Pitiless God, Thou alone hast managed all.
Thou, flattering me with an easy vengeance,
Hast twenty times daily opposed me to myself...
May he reign, this son...
May he be led to sink the knife in my breast.

It is Athalie herself, in this single line, who tells most directly of her murder.

Joas' final speech, and the only one he is given after his deed, is much shorter, only two couplets long. In it he assimilates something like Athalie's own vacillation to voice a prayer that he meet what was her fate if he turns out to imitate her (though at the same time he does not name her):

> *Dieu, qui voyez mon trouble et mon affliction,*
> *Détournez loin de moi sa malédiction,*
> *Et ne souffrez jamais qu'elle soit accomplie.*
> *Faites que Joas meure avant qu'il vous oublie.*
>
> (V,7)

God, you who see my trouble and affliction,
Deflect away from me his malediction
And suffer that it never be fulfilled.
Make Joas die before he may forget you.

The end here is too expected, in so far as the good is expected to triumph. We are very far from Aristotle's canons against simple poetic justice. At the same time it is also too simply unexpected, too little justified. The justification exists in the pious situation, but how is Racine able to make a tragedy out of merely pious gestures?

One answer as to how this pious fable may be taken for profound resides in the ambivalences that are being managed in the simplifications of the play. Among these ambivalences is the tension of progressive action between the horror of the murder, a kind of counterweight to facile piety, and the destined consummation the providential setting assumes, a forced simplification. The play is simplified, not simple, and to throw such questions onto this particular private religious stage required what was (already) an imagination of high order.

These answers are evasive. What sense do we have of revelation, of cathartic interaction, in this play? Another answer would look at the scenes themselves, curiously devoid of struggle within. This is true even of the lengthy encounter (II,7) of our chief antagonists, their only meeting in the play. She knows him not as a descendent but as the boy of her dreams; he knows her not as a forebear but only as the source of evil in his world. For the moment she intends not to stifle him but only to bring him to her palace. She has to mean what she says, and her statements cannot be taken for duplicity. He means only what he says, and his answers cannot be taken for effrontery. What they are on his side, as it turns out, is a royal confidence known to us through irony at this point because we know who he is. Her proposals we also know to be a desperate expedient. But nobody on stage knows that. We again are in the position of God (if we are adults), and the result in that sense is too unevolvedly foreknown. From that position we extrapolate the uncertainties and limitations of both speakers into the larger design of providence (what we wish); we likewise, concurrently, extrapolate the Sunday-school responses of the girls of Saint-Cyr into that larger design (how we handle our horror). Here is much of the encounter:

ATHALIE
   Vous pourrez le prier.
JOAS
   Je verrais cependant en invoquer un autre?
ATHALIE
   J'ai mon Dieu que je sers; vous servirez le vôtre.
   Ce sont deux puissants dieux.
JOAS
   Il faut craindre le mien:
   Lui seul est Dieu, Madame, et le vôtre n'est rien.
ATHALIE
   Les plaisirs près de moi vous chercheront en foule.
JOAS
   Le bonheur des méchants comme un torrent s'écoule.

ATHALIE
>Ces méchants, qui sont-ils?

JOSABET
>Hé, Madame! excusez.
>
>Un enfant...

ATHALIE (à Josabet)
>J'aime à voir comme vous l'instruisez
>Enfin, Eliacin, vous avez su me plaire;
>Vous n'êtes point sans doute un enfant ordinaire.
>Vous voyez, je suis reine, et n'ai point d'héritier.
>Laissez là cet habit, quittez ce vil métier.
>Je veux vous faire part de toutes mes richesses;
>Essayez dès ce jour l'effet de mes promesses.
>A ma table, partout, à mes côtés assis,
>Je prétends vous traiter comme mon propre fils.

JOAS
>Comme votre fils?

ATHALIE
>Oui. Vous vous taisez?

JOAS
>Quel père
>Je quitterais! Et pour...

ATHALIE
>Hé bien?

JOAS
>Pour quelle mère!

ATHALIE (à Josabet)
>Sa mémoire est fidèle, et dans tout ce qu'il dit
>De vous et de Joad je reconnais l'esprit.
>Voilà comme infectant cette simple jeunesse,
>Vous employez tous deux le calme où je vous laisse.
>Vous cultivez déjà leur haine et leur fureur;
>Vous ne leur prononcez mon nom qu'avec horreur.

JOSABET
>Peut-on de nos malheurs leur dérober l'histoire?
>Tout l'univers les sait; vous-même en faites gloire.

ATHALIE
> *Oui, ma juste fureur, et j'en fais vanité,*
> *A vengé mes parents sur ma posterité...*
> *David m'est en horreur; et les fils de ce roi,*
> *Quoique nés de mon sang, sont étrangers pour moi.*

ATHALIE
You may pray to him.
JOAS
And should I then see another one invoked?
ATHALIE
I have my God that I serve. You will serve yours.
They are two powerful gods.
JOAS
Mine must be feared.
He alone is God, lady, and yours is nothing.
ATHALIE
The pleasures near me will seek you out in throngs.
JOAS
The bliss of the evil runs off like a torrent.
ATHALIE
Who are these evil ones?
JOSABET
Ah, lady, pardon.
A child...
ATHALIE (to Josabet)
I like to see the way you teach him.
At last, Eliacin, you have learned to please me;
You are doubtless no ordinary child.
You see, I am queen, and I have no heir.
Abandon this costume, quit this vile trade.
I want to make you share in all my riches;
Test from this moment the effect of my promises.
At my table, everywhere, seated at my side,
I declare I will treat you as my own son.

JOAS
  As your son?
ATHALIE
  Yes. You are silent?
JOAS
  What a father.
  I would leave! And for...
ATHALIE
  Well?
JOAS
  For what a mother!
ATHALIE (to Josabet)
  His memory's faithful, and in all he says
  I recognize the spirit of Joad and yourself.
  This is how the two of you use the calm
  I leave you in to infect this simple youth.
  You already cultivate their hate and fury
  And only with horror pronounce to them my name.
JOSABET
  Can one rob them of our misfortunes' history?
  The whole world knows them; You glory in them yourself.
ATHALIE
  Yes, my just fury, and I am vain about it,
  Has avenged my parents on my posterity.
  I hold David in horror; and the sons of this king,
  Though born of my own blood, are strangers to me.

The social roles here consist not only of the queen questioning a subject, but specifically of the high-born visitor
interrogating a pupil to see how he answers, a scene that must
have been familiar to the girls of Saint-Cyr, and that Madame
de Maintenon herself must have enacted. The answers are
satisfactory enough to produce the fairy godmother proposal
known in folk motif and also in the Bible, in the adoption of
Moses by Pharaoh's daughter. Athalie is giving herself over to

such enchantments, but Joas is not, and his refusal recalls her to the political basis of their relation in a series of enjambments and short caesurae which subject one Racinian couplet to deformations more extreme than perhaps any to be found elsewhere in his plays:

JOAS
    Comme votre fils?
ATHALIE
    Oui. Vous vous taisez?
JOAS
    Quel père
    Je quitterais! Et pour...
ATHALIE
    Hé bien?
JOAS
    Pour quelle mère!

    The statement to Josabet retains a calm and a politeness which treats the priest's wife not only as a mother but also as a woman of equally high birth. The reply, and its neat summary in a rounded couplet of what Joas has brokenly implied, releases Athalie to produce a justification which in logical or legalistic terms, those of vengeance, are after all the identical ones that Joas would produce if the play asked him to.
    It does not. It does not have to. His justification is emotional; it resides in the peace and calm of an internal conviction that carries all before it, that audience and this audience. In her mouth, since she is damned, she can only rage. In his mouth, he is providential and will use vacillation only to utter a prayer. In this sense the play takes a quasi-Calvinistic attitude toward predestination and projects it back on the Old Testament, much as Jansenius, in the views of his attackers, had projected one onto St. Augustine.

Here, interestingly, the management of responses does not
extrapolate into forceful doctrines expressed by the characters,
as usually in the work of great tragedians. Moreover, the core
story does not provide—stories in themselves never provide—
the sort of implicit justification the philosopher demands.
What stories in themselves may provide is emotional overtone,
the mythic complexity; but this story, in being pietistic, is sub-
mythic. Athalie is a blank after as well as before the play.
The undiluted presentation of psychological material is called
not mythopoeia but sentimentalism, and this play, if it were
just addressed to the girls of Saint-Cyr, or just addressed to us,
would be sentimental. It is not: it subjects mere piety to a
refining process, and holds mere sentiment, its psychic material,
in the check precisely of piety toward the "history" of Israel,
toward this (imagined) event. It manages not just our ambivalent expectations, but also the interactions between those
expectations and the simplest expression of them, between
wisdom and piety, between the religion of the Grand Arnauld
and the automatic devotion of the girls of Saint-Cyr. The fusion,
trans-Jansenistic, is not explicitly Catholic: it is not, in fact,
theological. It is merely dramatic, it is dramatic in a "pure"-
form which Lionel Abel senses in the very act of singling this
one out among not just Racine's plays but among tragedies in
general.[26] *Athalie* offers a lowest common denominator of
tragedy, just by virtue of its simplifications. It escapes Madame
de Maintenon, and escapes the king himself, who is said to have
been nearly alone at the initial performance, and to have expressed a rage that the deprivation of costume and decor would
not fully carry. It escapes to us, it retains those ideal responses
that should have been, even if they were not in fact, the responses of the king, to whose situation the play is linked, both
directly as a spectator and indirectly as the husband of the
woman who made the request on behalf of the captive audience,
her young charges. To him and to her, but above all to them,
Saint-Cyr is the filter through which these commonplaces
become tragedy.

Or almost tragedy. All these sleights do not quite amount to the splendid enactment of *Phèdre*. *Athalie* finally pays a price for its simplicities, gained at whatever cost. The pietistic, when qualified, remains pietistic. The echo in the poetry is only an echo. Our play is less than *Phèdre*, as *Der Kaukasische Kreidekreis* is less than *Mutter Courage*, and for comparable reasons. Whatever the leverage, whatever the mastery, whatever the doctrine, Agit-prop remains limited in its ends. Drama triumphs over such limits because finally its ends are ineffable, as its effects are ineffaceable. *Esther*, like the *Cantiques Spirituels*, is mere Agit-prop. In *Athalie* Racine, like Brecht, has managed to bend Agit-prop toward dramatic ends. *Compassion* and *terreur*, though muted, are still operative enough to make the spectator of *Athalie* aware of the force behind half-managed ambivalences.

Chapter Three

TENDER RACINE

1

Cruel Racine is tender Racine. Relentlessly stripping actions
to their emotional essentials, Racine produces an effect of
cruelty, a cruelty that lays tenderness bare. Owning tenderness,
at the extreme, exposes a person to cruelty; and tragedy deals
with extremes. Yet in this tragic plenum, where rarely do
inessentials occupy psychological space, tenderness outfaces
cruelty, offering an emotional correlative for the process by
which idealism outfaces mortality.

Emotions are naked, to begin with, and of all the emotions
the nakedest is a love that transpires to any observer:

> L'amour n'est pas un feu qu'on renferme en une âme:
> Tout nous trahit, la voix, la silence, les yeux;
> Et les feux mal couverts n'en éclatent que mieux.
>
> (*Andromaque*, II,2)

> Love is no fire to enclose in a soul:
> All betrays us—voice, silence, eyes;
> And ill-covered fires only burst out the more.

Néron sadistically uses this principle to give vent to his jealousy.
When he thus forces Junie to pretend to banish Britannicus it
takes every jot of her love to conceal her love, and still the
concealment can last only for one moment. The lovers, for all
the fated risks they are taking, cannot help coming together

before their demise. Hippolyte, who evades his confidant's question about Aricie, must break his silence in the face of the woman herself. She in turn, under the same intense pressure of confronting a beloved, finds a way to dress her own nakedness of reciprocation in a tender modesty:

> *J'accepte tous les dons que vous me voulez faire.*
> *Mais cet Empire enfin si grand, si glorieux,*
> *N'est pas de vos présents le plus cher à mes yeux.*
> (*Phèdre*, II,3)

> I accept all the gifts you wish to make me,
> But this Empire at last so great, so glorious,
> Is not of your presents the dearest to my eyes.

In this visible nakedness of passion, exposure relentlessly leads to further exposure. Atalide fatally fails to conceal her love for Bajazet from her infuriated rival Roxane, unleashing a power that Roxane's own exposure keeps her from being able to use. So her vacillations kill her beloved, as Hermione's do Pyrrhus and Thésée's Hippolyte.

As so often, then, the critics' debate between tenderness and cruelty separates into antinomic poles what in the unified progress of a play constitutes a pure and total effect. Stressing cruelty strips a character's tenderness even further than Racine has done, since it divests him of the ultimate self-consistent devotion of idealism-in-love for which ultimately he is willing to die. Stressing tenderness undermines the action, saps the character of his committed morality, and turns tragedy into lyric effusion.

But it is tenderness, finally, that triumphs over mortality. A merely racked, merely evil Phèdre would not have been capable of her final confession, of honor-preserving suicide, overriding a Christian commandment, for a Christian audience.

Racine's tenderness perilously poises his plenum beyond the ? ambivalences out of which he builds his play: between religiosity and theatricality for the stage; between power and love, honor and power, honor and love for the action on a stage. The sheer, undeviating strand of tenderness, the "compassion" of which he speaks in the prefaces, serves to turn the unities into a calculus (the mathematical analogy being perhaps licensed by the relation of Pascal, his predecessor at Port-Royal, to this kind of thinking).

Piety in *Athalie* offers only a weak version; and destiny, even religious destiny, is a poor substitute for love. That emotion, and not the givens of his intellectual position or social situation toward the Spectator God of Goldmann, allows him to make the unities he had received from his tradition "une nécessité interne de l'oeuvre."[27] It would be possible to carry out a "refus du monde et de la vie," without being at all subject to passion: Pascal, who paradoxically did so in Goldmann's description, still could not have been the subject of a tragedy by Racine, nor could the account of his life produce the sense of purified time to which the impassioned Racinian hero moves over and over again in his plenum "pour la dernière fois."

The audience, and the playwright, are Christian; that ambivalence, between their own absolute values and the pre-Christian absolutes of tenderness, does constrict the action of Racine's plays into a kind of Renaissance equivalent for a modern Catholic-Freudian position. For the latter, the commandment to love one's enemies, in the face of the primal emotional dialectic that allows hostility to be sublimated or distorted but not annihilated, is either dangerous (unwitting masochism) or heroic (the slow redemption of repression into sublimation, or id into ego). The most difficult area for the exercise of this commandment is precisely the area of Racine's preoccupation, the erotic passions. The compelling and all-embracing elements of those passions may be heroically managed, but the elements remain the same. The enemy within the erotic sphere, the successful rival, cannot within that sphere be loved; and even if the heroic Christian commandment manages to sublimate the hostility toward the neighbor rival, that hostility remains as the element that is being heroically managed. Antiochus can at best keep himself in check toward Titus. Roxane's long friendship for Atalide, like Iphigénie's for Eriphile, dissolves in the very instant the shadow of rivalry is discerned. Phèdre has even at the very end no good word for Aricie—though she does condemn (IV,6) the impulse that would "perdre" that rival. Thésée vacillates at tragic lengths in this primal reaction to Phèdre's accusation against his son. In *Mithridate*, too, the rival is a son, and a real rival; a son who has earlier proved his devotion by repudiating his own mother in the father's favor. And still it takes the whole play and the approach of death for the aging king to accept his son's rivalry.

Mithridate surrenders the woman he loves not through any idealism *naturaliter Christiana*, but in response to the other natural element of human life—he is aging; and through response to the other sphere of natural affection: it is in favor of a son that he surrenders.

In this sense, Racine would be betraying his faith as well as his convictions to sentimentalize those convictions by "forgetting" them in favor of a saccharine pietism. Committing himself to the plenum of the passionate elements in his plays, Racine is most Christian when he is least "Christian": is most faithful to the power of human devotion when he presents the elements of that devotion in unqualified, non-Christian nakedness.

When the tender orphan in him finally surrenders to the flattering courtier, in an unimaginable ten years of what he calls *un siècle si pervers*,[28] the court extracts from their new zombie of mere pietism the grisly spectacle of an envisioned passion sacrificed to a jejune sanctimoniousness: the author of *Phèdre* consents to write *Esther* for society girls in the queen's favorite nunnery school. That piece of royal flattery and standard, automatic religiosity, stays on the terrain of eroticism without invoking more than a calculated use of erotic appeal. Esther's attraction merely furthers the ends of a Persian despotism seen as benevolent in a way that the biblical

book of Esther never expounds: the career of Madame de
Maintenon, so to speak, is flattered along with the career of the
Roi Soleil (whose own favorite play remained *Mithridate*).[29]
Even the *Thébaide* and *Alexandre* surpass *Esther*. Stale in the
theatre, the play is a horror in the life of its transmogrified
author. The knives of worldliness have scarred the orphan, and
it is only by reinventing a biblical context in *Athalie*, not
merely staging one, and finally by getting out of the erotic
sphere entirely, that he can successfully present a Christian
view of power, personifying the Old Testament national elec-
tion in an orphan scarred by knives. *Athalie*, neatly, is rejected
by both the court, which cancelled the full-scale production,
and the church, which took offense at it. When cruelty mutes
tenderness in favor of destiny, compassion and terror are sapped.
And, as it happens, no one was satisfied—except perhaps the
self-deceiving author and his pious posterity.

2

In the plenum with which every word of Racine's best plays
resounds, there is a loss at the heart, the tragic gap of the old
Racinian formula, A loves B, but B loves C, who loves. ... Passion builds a plenum of paradise where A would love B and B
would love A, rounded and growing into an expansive perfec-
tion that is only yearned for. On his stage, paradise has been
lost, passion is unpredictable, and the proportions of the
equation open towards further loss. If, when A loves B, it
happens that B loves C, then each becomes a problem as well
as an obsession for the other. It can be so even when the love is
shared, if power threatens a separation from above, as in *Britannicus*, and *Bajazet*, and *Mithridate*, or from outside the self
and within the duty to those outside, as in *Bérénice*.
    The situation, given the sense of love within, or from without,
is at once static, seen as a plenum, and dynamic, seen as an
effort to institute one. In *Andromaque*, the static forces of the

plenum, even before the play opens, have gone through the
same round again and again, as Pylade tells Oreste in the very
opening:

Et chaque jour encore on lui voit tout tenter
Pour fléchir sa captive, ou pour l'épouvanter.
De son fils, qu'il lui cache, il menace la tête,
Et fait couler des pleurs, qu'aussitôt il arrête.
Hermione elle-même a vu plus de cent fois
Cet amant irrité revenir sous ses lois,
Et de ses voeux troublés lui rapportant l'hommage,
Soupirer à ses pieds moins d'amour que de rage.

(I,1)

And daily they see him still try everything
To bend his captive or alarm her.
He threatens the head of her son, whom he hides,
And makes those tears flow that he stops at once.
Hermione herself has seen more than a hundred times
This disturbed lover come back under her sway
And, bringing her homage of his troubled vows,
Sigh at her feet less out of love than rage.

A static sense persists: Pyrrhus, Hermione, and Andromaque
act no differently; all through the play we see than in this
description—except that Oreste, introduced in their midst with
political pressure for Pyrrhus and amorous devotion for Hermione, causes the patterned interactions this time to generate
a dynamism. This will complicate his pressure and his devotion,
producing sorrowful transmutations for everyone.

For all the transparency of everyone to everyone else, for
all Pylade's exact sense of the special contour of repetitions in
the vacillation, for all Oreste's willingness to murder a king at
his own altar and Andromaque's willingness to go through a
marriage she will die rather than honor (in order to have the
new husband honor the promise to leave her son alive), for all

Pyrrhus' diplomatic mastery between the complications of two wrought women and the demands of his fellow Greeks—for all this, the play, in producing the transforming plenum of the end, magnifies every complex condition of its outset. Everyone seemed statically accounted for, the resilient and impassioned quartet seemed to deploy all the known forces. And yet as the dynamic lightning strikes, after Act 4, everyone is given not only something he did not expect but even something different from the alternatives he had sensibly laid out according to the enclosed and total conditions of the play: Pyrrhus, who thought he would be marrying either Andromaque or Hermione, is killed at the hands of Oreste. Oreste, who thought he would be rewarded by a Hermione who might or might not love him for murdering her unfaithful lover, finds himself abandoned by her totally and pursued anew by the Furies, who are identified with his beloved. Hermione, who thought herself to have either Pyrrhus or revenge, finds an impulsive suicide after confronting the bloody corpse. And Andromaque, who expected either death for her son and herself or else a complicated death to save his life, finds herself once more the widow performing over again the necessary duties for her dead husband. The conditions of the plenum seem perfect for foresight. And indeed the prudent Pylade's summary in the opening, as quoted above, is faithful to all the motions of the play—except the outcome. The prudence of Pylade, and of the confidants generally in these plays, is powerless, even when the confidant is also a deeply devoted friend (Oenone), a sage courtier (Acomat), a fellow ruler (Antiochus), or an unscrupulous manipulator (Narcisse): prudence can summarize but not compass the plenum of passion, and these characters stand to one side as the passive confidants of the impassioned. They, the principals, move in their terrible figures alone, turning all their reactions and powers to the single service that will undo them.

   In this shared plenum, the involvement of everyone impassioned is equal because it is total: there are no "protagonists" and "deuteragonists." Antiochus is really as important as

Titus, who is as important as Bérénice. Thésée is as important as Phèdre or Hippolyte, Agamemnon or Eriphile as Iphigénie. It took Racine a while to learn this; the two plays of his apprenticeship set forth a central passion but fail to make it a plenum because they follow the age-old tradition of centering on a single figure. In the *Thébaide*, all the evil is located in one person, Créon, and the youthful Racine finds an outlet towards a formulaic, bastard plenum by having him fall in love with the Antigone who loves his son! She is thus a Junie and a Monime towards him, as well as being an Atalide to Hémon and an Andromaque to Polynice. Yet all her condensation, so to speak, of his later heroines seems only uncertainty: the play has not created the psychological space for the forces themselves to condense. In *Alexandre*, likewise, that conqueror is too dominant and magnanimous a figure to allow the full development that the ensuing *Andromaque* sets forth. As Racine himself says in his preface to *La Thébaide*, the play is "plutôt l'ouvrage d'un déclamateur, qui ne savait ce que c'était que tragédie."

3

The tension between equal selves on stage draws them into an unequal attempt to master the space, to achieve the sensed but radically elusive plenum of fusing power and love. The attempt produces, against the even progress of the lines and the set stances of the personages, a faltering progress of fits and starts, tremendous, nearly successful efforts and bypassing failures. These *diminuendi* and *crescendi* modulate the Racinian music or else hold it at the pitch of constantly expected modulation—the massive change of voice and mood, tempo and loudness which the elocutionary style of the Comédie-Française serves so well, and which provides it with the occasion for its greatest triumphs. At its most extreme, the vacillation operates so powerfully that it swings between one alternative and the other. Here, for example, Hermione changes her stance every line or two, pulled as she is between saving her lover and satisfying her jealousy by the given order for Pyrrhus' death:

Où suis-je? Qu'ai je fait? Que dois-je faire encore?
Quel transport me saisit? Quel chagrin me dévore?
Errante, et sans dessein, je cours dans ce palais.
Ah! ne puis-je savoir si j'aime, ou si je hais?
Le cruel! de quel oeil il m'a congédiée!
Sans pitié, sans douleur, au moins étudiée.
L'ai-je vu se troubler et me plaindre un moment?
En ai-je pu tirer un seul gémissement?
Muet à mes soupirs, tranquille à mes alarmes,
Semblait-il seulement qu'il eût part à mes larmes?
Et je le plains encore? Et pour comble d'ennui
Mon coeur, mon lâche coeur s'intéresse pour lui?
Je tremble au seul penser du coup qui le menace? ...
Il me laisse, l'ingrat! cet embarras funeste.
Non, non encore un coup: laissons agir Oreste.
Qu'il meure, puisqu'enfin il a dû le prévoir,
Et puisqu'il m'a forcée enfin à le vouloir.
A le vouloir? Hé quoi? C'est donc moi qui l'ordonne?
Sa mort sera l'effet de l'amour d'Hermione?...
L'assassiner, le perdre? Ah! devant qu'il expire...
                                              (V,1)

Where am I? What have I done? What more must I do?
What transort grips me, what distress devours me?
Wandering aimlessly I run through this palace.
Ah, can I not know if I love or hate?
Cruel man! With what a look he sent me off!
Without pity, without sorrow, studied at least.
Have I seen him one time take pains and weep for me?
Could I draw out of him a single moan?
Mute to my sighs, tranquil to my alarms,
Did he even seem to share in my tears?

Do I still weep for him?, and as a last annoyance,
Does my heart, my coward heart, respond to him?
I tremble at the sole thought of a blow threatening him?
He leaves me, the ingrate, this dire perplexity.
No, no, another blow: let Oreste act.
May he die, since at last he should have foreseen it,
And since he at last forced me to wish it!
To wish it? What? Is it I who order that?
The cause of his death will be Hermione's love?
To kill him, to lose him? Ah, before he dies...

The tightness of the play draws Oreste and Hermione towards confrontation. Dialogue between two persons is the normative interaction on the stage of Racine, but rarely—so heavily are the speakers overmastered by this tense verbal vacillation—do they stand up squarely against one another for the even interchange of the stichometry that often dominates Racine's Greek models. Even in the tightest of Racine's plays, in *Bérénice*, he gives its pitched trio right through the end just enough latitude to vacillate inwardly under the cruelly revealed pressures of tenderness.

Bérénice stands up for the final speech of an occasion that forces her to modulate her address (1) to both suitors, (2) to Titus, then (3) to Antiochus, then (4) to Titus again. In the first she is the magnanimous advocate against the "désespoir" her phrasing indicates she may be sharing with them:

Partout du désespoir je rencontre l'image.

(V,7)

I meet the image everywhere of despair.

In the second, the longest of the four, she renounces Rome, then shades into saying that her knowledge of Titus' love consoles her for her loss (the opposite of what she had maintained to him in Act 5, Scene 5, "Ah, cruel! par pitié, montrez moi moins d'amour"). The third speech, to Antiochus, allows her to transpire with all the calm she had begun to show in the first. And in the fourth she cannot help saying again to Titus what she had already said, "Pour la dernière fois, adieu, Seigneur." Titus to all this can say nothing at all, and Antiochus only "Hélas!" The end of plenitude is a silence in which the three separate forever, after racking their language to the end on the tension of the impossible demands made upon them. The plenum requires action as well as measured words: it requires the stipulated and mortally threatened equality of the characters, two conditions that *Alexandre* does not fulfill, while it does already have the Racinian language.

The loss in the plenum governs the large motions from scene to scene as well as the small motions from one part of a speech to another. As the submission of *gloire* to *amour* and *honneur* to *passion* works out its logic, the characters who remain equal to each other are unequal to the consistency their very amorous vision of a paradisiacal plenum demands from them. The geometry of time thus works against them too: the inequality is bound to make itself more visible as the vision of the plenum recedes with every scene.

Antiochus opens *Bérénice* by announcing his intention to tell her (I,1) what he does not tell Titus till the close of the play. His announcement (I,2) comes in the form of a series of vacillating questions to himself which end by silencing the announcement. And still he must face the Bérénice before whom he has been silent five years ("d'un voile d'amitié j'ai couvert mon amour"). He has decided to announce his departure "à jamais" to the other end of the world, from which they have both come; and he must serve instead (I,4) as the confidant of her love for his rival; and even as its honorable helper— a pressure which brings him indeed, and finally, to his declaration:

> *Je me suis tu cinq ans,*
> *Madame, et vais encor me taire plus longtemps.*

De mon heureux rival j'accompagnai les armes;
J'espérai de verser mon sang après mes larmes...
Vous pleurâtes ma mort, hélas! trop peu certaine.

I have kept still five years,
Lady, and even longer will keep still.
I went along with my happy rival's arms.
I hoped to shed my blood after my tears....
You would weep my death, alas! too little certain.

which evokes from her—what else can it when she loves another?—
the cruelty of mere kindness calling him back to the *amitié*
it had been such torture for him to maintain. And when he
leaves (I,5) she is shocked that her maid suggests she might
have retained him and thereby flattered an "ardeur insensée."
What she turns away to is the rift in her own situation, something she will not face and the confidante Phénice forces her to
face; "Rome hait tous les rois, et Bérénice est reine." The act
closes with her statement of a disbelief her earlier speeches had
shown her to be entertaining in spite of herself.

The hidden emperor appears in Act 2 to face the popular
qualifications of his love, with a masculine directness and a
lover's sorrow; he is torn as he is asked to abandon that love:

Un héros vainqueur de tant de nations
Saurait bien, tôt ou tard, vaincre ses passions.
(II,2)

A hero who has conquered so many nations
Could well, soon or late, conquer his passions.

"Ah! que sous de beaux noms cette gloire est cruelle!" Titus
says, draining off the impossibility of his regret in the exclama-
tions that begin and end this sentence, that punctuate insistently the rhetorical questions and gropings of the following
speeches (II,2). He not only totters but speaks of tottering.

N'y songeons plus. Allons, cher Paulin: plus j'y pense,
Plus je sens chanceler ma cruelle constance.

Dream of it no more. Come, Paulin: the more I think
  of it
The more I feel waver my cruel constancy.

He is then forced at once to confront Bérénice (II,4); her
presence, above all her "bontés," bring him to a silence, "je
ne lui puis rien dire." Still, his very silence ominously presses
her to face the question she has been evading, the possibility
of an emperor's not being able to marry a foreign queen. But
the lover explains away the vacillations of the beloved; he
succeeds in reestablishing a precarious evasion all over again.

At the beginning of the third act, Titus, in desperation at
his own silence, pleads with their common friend Antiochus
to assume the burden, new for him, of carrying to the queen
the word Antiochus knows will make her hate him without
detaching her affections from Titus (III,2), though the request
(III,1) comes in the form that Antiochus perform what he most
desires and most despairs of, that he himself marry Bérénice.
But he does transmit his message (III,3) and is rewarded with
Bérénice's command that he never again set eyes on her; to
which he responds by deciding again he will leave (III,4), and
stays.

After some staccato preparations, Titus now finds himself
alone before a departing Bérénice, whom he easily delays to
engage in the mutual pain of contemplating a separation. For
this she finds it easy to blame him and difficult to sustain the
motions of doing so (IV,5). Her final revenge will be the effect
she knows his love for her will have on him! (She relies on the
plenum and is not consoled.) The prospect of this drives him to
think of suicide; to share the thought with her impels the final
separation: the drive towards a plenum vacates its possibility.
The actualization of the vacancy occupies the actors, who waver
along the relentless course of a descending spiral, propelled by

nothing other than the best of their ideals in inexorable conflict with the best of their desires. At every point their words will strain to come to terms with the conflicting demands of ideals that would seem to fortify one another, honor and love. The plenum is enacted, and vanishes, as the play exacts and exhibits the mightiness of the vacillations toward it.

4

In the normal social interchange of language between auditor and speaker, the code is based on the condition that the two may reverse roles freely through dialogue. In dialogue across the stage barrier between the composite, represented "speaker," the actors on stage, and the collective "auditor," the persons in the audience, this condition of free role reversal is suspended. Caught in an uninterrupted silence much the way the analysand is committed to uninterrupted speech, the auditor is thrown into a pure sequence of feeling that the language of the play structures for him. He can never become a speaker; and even a silent person on stage must be accounted a "speaker" and not an auditor.

Thus in the theater the doubled speech act is unified; only one of the auditor-speaker partners may speak. And at the same time the spectator's unified world is doubled: normally he moves in one open terrain, but here he enters a large, darkened room where he looks in on another, doubled audience-world across whose barrier he may not cross. In the theater of Racine this doubling-unification finds a correlative and mirror not only in the form of the verse, with its unified doublings and doubled unities of couplet in caesural alexandrine, but also in a staged version of the normal speaker-auditor interchange. In real life, the rudimentary exchange of speech is a two-way one; on Racine's stage it is between two persons who are in the primal relation of love, or else of its inverse, rivalry-hatred. All the encounters follow this pattern, when the principals are not trying to muster their resources with a confidant for facing such an encounter—in which case the self is doubled with another who is reflexive, but who never exhibits the occasionally full subordination of the Shakespearian or Sophoclean servant.

Purified on stage is an attempt to master through formal language the encounter that reigns also over the psychodynamic economy in the real world of the person watching: he too reacts to single encounters in primary love or primary hatred, though in the later Freudian reading, as never in the simplicity of Racine's tenderness, love has an underside of potential hostility, hostility an underside of repressed love. In Racine, then, the encounter that dominates is the two-way one. The forces natural to each of the sexes—the woman's demand for honorable fidelity that Mauron traces,[30] the man's decisiveness—combine, like every other attribute, to intensify the suprasexual, human drive for erotic fulfillment. Beside this primary drive, all natural attributes of sex or traits of character are secondary.

And in Racine, as in the Oedipal economy, the tragic loss derives not from a cosmic special destiny or from the labyrinths of character. The main personages have character only as a secondary network of response: primarily they all act alike. As in the Oedipal economy, the problem consists of the tragic splitting between past (mother or Phèdre) and present (son, seeking some present love goal, Hippolyte and Aricie), or between the two-way force of love (the mother loves the son; or Pyrrhus, whose father killed her husband, loves Andromaque) and the intrusion, inevitably, of complicating third parties who introduce their own two-way desires (the father; or Hector is dead actually but alive for Andromaque; or Hermione also loves Pyrrhus and has him killed in spite of herself when he does not respond).

The Racinian love diagram, then, corresponds to a primary psychograph, one that for the seventeenth century audience we become when we watch it is as much of a given as the

Freudian one for the modern audience. The diagram is worked out across the stage barrier, hitting home beyond irony and serenities, in long speeches whose effect Madame de Sevigné speaks of as a "shuddering," "ces tirades...qui font frissonner."[31]

The primal scene on Racine's stage is stripped down to primal elements: it is subjected to the "unities" that his literary-linguistic superego transmitted to him from the ideal, other past of a classical Greece uncomplicated with the God-orientation of his superego in the action of the world. The space is a bare one through which people pass: in *Andromaque* an indifferent palace room, as in *Britannicus*: in the vestibule of *Athalie*, Agamemnon's tent in *Iphigénie*, an indifferent part of the Seraglio in *Bajazet*, in *Mithridate* and *Phèdre* at an unde-fined spot in or before a palace. In *Bérénice*, it is a space located between the apartment of Titus and that of Bérénice.

Everything is rendered simple, space and language and personnel, for working out upon the audience the purified time-dynamic of the tragic diagram. The gradual, regular, and inexorable vacating of the plenum is envisioned through and because of the even logic of its disappearance. Between the glad Oreste who meets Pylade in the first scene of *Andromaque* and the maddened one whom Pylade saves in spite of himself at the end of the play, there are the deaths whose sacrifice occurs because of immersion and not because of flaws or errors. Oreste goes from the plenum of "Oui, puisque je re-trouve un ami si fidèle" to the vacancy of his last words, "Et je lui porte enfin mon coeur à dévorer." But Pylade has the very last words of the play, those of a restoring idealism:

> *Sauvons-le. Nos efforts deviendrait impuissants*
> *S'il reprenait ici sa rage avec ses sens.*
>
>   (V,5)

Let's save him. Our efforts would be powerless
If he got back his rage here with his sense.

The love, at once erotic and courtly, that propels Racine's characters is itself presented to the spectator as a given, not a problem. There is none of Dante's vast exploration of its meaning, none of Wagner's or Claudel's profound celebration of its exaltations. The ultimate value which leads those supreme artists to transcendent representations is for Racine only accepted and incorporated. The fires are more banked for not being given their inflammatory course. The love appears full-blown, undeviating, an all-embracing fact of existence. The sense and the guarantee of the plenum is made to appear exclusively, and therefore purely, in the very limitations that exact its loss.

In this sense, in the calm and heroic acceptance of the given tenderness, with all its depths, Racine approaches, much more than in his intellectual position towards power or official religion, the condition for his theatre of the "spectator God" that Goldmann attributes to him.[32] This notion, which Goldmann applies at three removes through Mère Angelique's quotation of it from St. Augustine, may be applied most fully to *Athalie*, where the adult audience, deflecting through the audience of edified little girls, may be stated as significantly congruous with the God before whom the Old Testament figures played out their involvements. For Racine's "secular" tragedies, the question is more complicated because he is careful (as Corneille is not) to keep his characters, from modern history or ancient history or myth, in a non-Christian world. He is also careful never to present any kind of explicitly religious values as other than a last resort for the time after the action—just one time in Junie's cloistering; or to make sacrifice a result of passion and not devotion, just one time in the Eriphile of *Iphigénie*; or to make self-immolation a classical gesture towards honor for a god who is spoken of as an ancestor and the sun, just one time in *Phèdre*.

The passion links to the economy of human life, first by being the most intense form of the basic two-person interaction or dialogue. Erotic passion, moreover, is the area where the distinction between self and other is most total, since the deepest reciprocation is necessary for fulfillment. It is also most nullified, since the plenum envisioned and never realized is one which all the struggle and partiality that impels dialogue between self and other would be conceived of as melted away in a plenum of perpetual (here unattainable) transport. This condition of Eros is still more an equivalent for the Jansenist crux between predestination and grace (love is destined, and necessary for happy survival, and an ineffable gift) than it is for Descartes' *Traité des Passions.*[33] In the world of Jansenist theology, the argument is an intellectual one; it is unresolvable because the weight to be given the element under determination (say, grace) is dependent on the other and indeterminate factor (say, predestination). On Racine's stage, the ambivalences by recreating an implied ambivalence in the analogous sphere of the profane passion. That passion is never justified, only taken for granted as a tragic, and all-embracing reality, for those on stage who are caught in its logic; for those in the audience, who may assimilate the logic and reap the perception of tenderness without going under to its qualifications.

Since religion has been excluded from the plays for a formally devoted audience and for a playwright who retained his office and income of *prieur* until 1674,[34] the real world is by verbal definition larger than the world on stage: the condensation and displacements imply the uncondensed and undisplaced.

Of the ambivalent elements that he condenses in his work, religious devotion is the most marginal, exposed only at the far end of a play or in the brief effusion of an appeal to a god muted through such classicized but by no means classical figures as fictionalizing-by-pluralization (*dieux*) or obnubilation-by-metonymy (*Ciel*).

It is, paradoxically, the very absence of religious questions from the plays which permits the assimilation of the honor-qualified and honor-exhibiting tenderness into a religious sphere. The spectator, having been bound away from his own world of religious devotion, is then freed for the connections that, so to speak, Dante or Claudel make for him. Racine's theatrical effect offers not a total world view but a partial, and powerful corrective: elements that press for acknowledgement of their inexorable coherence. This Carte du Tendre, because its boundaries are so effectively set, may be taken to evoke emotionally the possibility of a larger cosmos, one of equally compelling clarity. So its urgency demands that we feel.

Chapter Four

THE PASTNESS OF POWER

The love to which Racine's characters are ultimately subjected and in which they locate their other ideals—predominantly if not "sans contre-poids" in Suarès' phrase—is itself
seen on his stage differently from the unambivalent description that the *prieur* Racine might have given.[35] But the power
to which his stage lovers are subjected in time is the same as
the power dominating his real world. The church changes the
soul; it does not change the constituted power of the ruler.
Unlike Corneille, however, Racine never has his characters do
homage to "empire" except in passing, or as an enhancement
to love when a woman like Hermione or Bérénice declares in
her transports that empire adds to her lover's basic appeal.
Racine's people exist in that royal absoluteness as the mem-
bers of his audience did, whose amorous existence might be
complicated by commandments to which he would himself
defer but whose public existence was simplified under the
Roi Soleil as Racine allowed his own to be simplified, after
exhibiting that even condition in play after play. From
Alexandre to Amurat in time, and from Rome to India in
space, the state authority centers in a single person who brings
that authority onto stage as one among many of the attributes which an equal and susceptible person may have, but to
which all the other persons must defer. Yet never does the
ruler in Racine's plays embody the splendid ideal of the Auguste
of *Cinna* or the remote benevolence of the king in the *Cid*.

This constituted power has been established in the past of the play. Only in *Alexandre*, where the connotations of the conqueror's name indicate the outcome, and only in *Bajazet*, where an amorous harem betrothed tries to substitute the king's brother for himself, is there any of the struggle over rule that dominate *Horace* and *Cinna*. In *Phèdre* the question does come up in the middle of the play as a shadow between the lovers, to unify Hippolyte with Aricie, and divide him from Phèdre, a question resolved by the reappearance of Thésée. Poulet stresses the power of pastness in Racine—against the Léon of Corneille who would free himself from the consequences of the past—citing the preface to *Bajazet*: "le respect que l'on a pour les héros augmente à mesure qu'ils s'éloignent de nous."[36] And past is connected with present, as Racine goes on to say: "L'esprit finit par ne plus apercevoir dans le déroulement sombre des choses, que leur interdépendance."[37]

Racine again unlike Corneille, felt in his prefaces the need to establish pastness. In all of his plays, he presents a situation that has received a cachet either from actual historiography (*Alexandre*, *Britannicus*, *Mithridate*, *Esther*, *Athalie* in his description, and *Bérénice*; and even the doubtful *Bajazet*, where he gives a first-hand, if questionable, oral authority for the events). Or else the cachet comes from not just myth, which the Greek playwright handled freely as Racine well knew, but from a handling of the myth sanctified by a lesser Greek than the great Sophocles he did not dare approach, by Euripides (*La Thébaide*, *Andromaque*, *Iphigénie*, *Phèdre*).

At the beginning of the preface to *Phèdre*, Racine proceeds without a paragraph break from justifying the play's source to adjudicating its moral. Just as the Racinian ruler is omnipotent and yet an equal person, so the past, which functions as a releasing justification, stands also on equal footing with the present it sponsors.

The constituted power of the Racinian third party who faces the lovers, derives not from a recent institution but from the past, and a past within the personal psychic economy

rather than a merely public equilibrium: the previous generation, most often the father, holds sway. The barrier between
generations even appears in Racine as an attenuated incest
taboo.[38] Mithridate, the Thésée of *Phèdre*, the Agamemnon of
Iphigénie govern the action by their presence or their absence,
in the case of Agamemnon by machinations of which he is
the victim as well as the misunderstood author. In *Bérénice*
an ancestral authority, in *Bajazet* an elder brother, in *Britannicus* an imperious mother against whom is pitted a Néron slightly
older than the doomed lovers, serve to dynamize the past as
the field of force upon which the love must operate. Moreover,
Britannicus is the foster brother, and also the brother-in-law,
of Néron. In *Andromaque* each of the four main agents is
mounting a prior family situation; Oreste is ravaged by the
judicial murder of his mother, the rope he is at the end of here;
Andromaque honors the commandments of a dead husband;
Hermione, caught in the shadow of her illustrious mother,
manipulates by obeying her father; Pyrrhus is caught in the
obligation to act as the true son of Achilles, the title by which
Oreste (I,2) greets him on his first appearance.

The force of the past does not stand uniformly over the
play. It is manipulated, it wavers, it is subjected and then it
dominates. The theme of the return of the father, as Baudouin[39]
and Mauron[40] point out, is a recurrent one in these plays.
Around a father's entrances and exits the illusion of change is
produced, and so is a reiteration of sameness: the situation is
only forced to go through the evolutions which are inevitable,
given the dispositions of the characters. It is impossible to
get beyond the duty to the father in *Mithridate*, as in the *Cid*;
but in Racine's plays the impossibility is resolved not by the
heroic idealization of the lovers but by the father himself,
who on another plane is the rival in love of the son he for-
gives. The past-become-present declares its own pastness;
Mithridate withdraws because he is aging.

In this play, as in *Phèdre*, the father's absence occurs in
its most extreme form: he is reported to be dead. The seeming

finality of the opening couplet of the play closes and rhymes on the announcement "Mithridate est mort." In the light of the report, both his sons, the "good" one Xipharès and the "bad" one Pharnace, who take the opposite positions about resistance to Rome (Xipharès had opposed his own mother on this point, supporting his father and conciliation), take the same position of suitor towards their father's long-standing fiancée Monime. She lets it be known that she shares the affection of the good son. When the father returns, everything depends on their concealing an affection the father's intriguing foxiness (in the attribute of the cliché "oriental despot," as well as in the infallible prescience of the Racinian lover) knows how to reveal. His forty-year boldness against the Romans is matched by a long-schooled alertness in his own court, the one policy he declares still at the very end of Act 3 he will continue to follow:

> *Dissimulons encor, comme j'ai commencé.*

> Dissimulate further, as I have begun.

But Xipharès, for all his goodness, is still his father's son, and he matches Mithridate in sensing the dissimulation ("J'ai lu dans ses regards sa prochaine vengeance." [IV,2]). The course of vengeance is broken by the false report of Xipharès' own death in Act 5, but that brief backtracking is halted, just in time to keep Monime from poisoning herself. She enters the father's living and undissimulated presence, to receive, in the final words of the father's now real death, the blessing that will unite them, to divide the son who is faithful in family and in empire from the son who had only seemed to be.

    Death, which can enter life at any time for the equal human being, is envisaged as a possibility from the beginning; so its cumulative effect is blunted at the end. It is only one among many possible seals upon the action. Pyrrhus happens to die, Andromaque and Oreste do not. If Hermione dies, she has chosen death out of an evil confusedness for which love is not wholly responsible. Iphigénie is ready to die, but Eriphile is more deeply ready to die, and she does. After the reported death of Thésée and the report of Hippolyte's real death, Phèdre can expire on stage as an honorable conclusion to her dishonor, and that event does not pull the action together, as do the deaths in the *Trachiniai* or the *Oedipus at Colonus*, or the *Hippolytus* of Euripides. Atalide's self-immolation is almost a by-blow of the oriental intrigue which has brought the dark Orcan to murder other principals. The killing of Athalie opens a providential royal succession.

Mortality occurs in a restricted field, and the play's uniform progression in time keeps it from really rounding out. *Compassion* and *terreur*, Racine's repeated terms for his "effect", not only intensify the pity and fear of Aristotle; they also refer to an effect of greater duration; the sense of the play is a *bon sens* and a *raison* mortality does not qualify.

The Racinian theorem offers no full enactment of life; in that limitation it differs from the presumed ambition of Aeschylus, Sophocles, and Euripides, as from Shakespeare's. Racine's audience, and the playwright himself, subscribe to values that transcend the play in matters other than love, and especially concerning the sense of death. It is not true that tragedy is radically unchristian; Shakespeare's plays, and the deaths in his plays, are rich in Christian complication, and the act of detaching him from his Christian involvements has exactly to start with those. But the Christian "good" death enters Racine's plays obliquely, in the appropriateness (consistency is beside the point) of Athalie's, the resolvedness of Phèdre's, the fatality of Eriphile's: her perversity deprives Eriphile of any positive analogy to the sainted martyr sensing her future. Racine's theorem offers only the past-bound elements of life, final and unresisting, with which the eschatological and theological imagination would have to deal. Racine demonstrates a Jansenist nature, against which the transcendent grace must operate to be effective: he offers extreme parables of determination, where death terminates without explanation. The death of Phèdre adds no sense to her passion, or to her own struggle against it: we had already seen both effectively.

The death, then, curiously, has a purer effect, and one more congruous with the delimited language and action of the play: it is unqualified, it offers no new term, it only puts into the full past the life that had been dominated by the partial past, it only proves the totality of a love whose totality we had seen operative at every step.

And concordantly, the past's power is only abstract, not mythic. For all the power, psychoanalytic as it were, of the family in Racine (which Freud has taught us to read in mythic patterns), for all his dependence on mythic situations, the mythic ambivalences are not given any rein in his plays. They are kept taut behind and around and before the play, so to speak, but not in the unremittingly abstract action. "Vénus tout entière à sa proie attachée" reveals none of the trans-cendences of the Euripidean Aphrodite, none of the philo-sophizing that Shakespeare's lovers explore. It is a given, and a single given.

The plots themselves, even when derived from myth, do not admit of mythic complication, but only of two-way action. All mediators, all the tragic intrusion of the third parties, serve only as a check on the essential, and abstract, confronta-tion. The mythic ambivalences, like the faith of the audience, are checked at the door of the theatre: to provide a kind of negative intensification in the simple strength of Racine's profound effect (they have to be harnessing the psychological forces that myths address in order to have any dramatic effect at all). Racine is not even willing to indulge the pyrotechnic displays of sentimental mythic horror characteristic of the plays of his contemporaries, who borrowed similar plots from antiquity.[41] He reduces his effect to the simplest terms. This practice itself obliges him to extend the complications of his situations backward, to exhibit the pastness of a power in the process of achieving another, tragic pastness. So do the lovers tend to fall away from their plenum into the "might have been" which is the amorous dimension, here tightly enacted, of man's invincible mortality.

Chapter Five

THE PRESENTNESS OF POWER

The play also extends its complications forward, as it must, reducing them to a simplicity of loss under the aegis of a power felt—for all its shifting—uniformly through the play. One event turns the screw of another. Oenone is silenced from immediate response to Phèdre's epochal confession by the immediate news of Thésée's death. Then, in turn, Phèdre's *"Ciel,"* when she hears the news, redounds with what Oenone spells out, the contingent possibilities for erotic development, residing in a common front against the third party contender Aricie. But Hippolyte already loves Aricie enough to discount her hostile past; to her, compoundingly, he has already broken silence; he has already declared himself to her just before he arrives to hear Phèdre's declaration.

Here, and everywhere, is a presentness of power, where *amour* dominates even the *empire* under which it must subsist, declare itself, conceal itself, struggle for improbable realization, and then, failing that, accept the Pyrrhic victory of a merely demonstrated honor. Under the pressure of the tragic complications, *amour* must lose out one way or another. In the tragic view only the maintained ideal of love can be said to win. Mithridate, king though he is, cannot bind an unloving betrothed. Phèdre is not guilty in act of either incest or adultery; she is guilty of desire. A desire to speak merely excruciates her at the beginning. To confess desire before an unscrupulous nurse is to unleash in herself the forces leading to downfall, by the logic of the passion itself. What has been named to one other cannot be concealed in the presence of the loved other himself, Hippolyte. His revulsion, dramatic in its consequences for himself, also unleashes the dramatic consequences of jealousy and shame in Phèdre, the emotions so encouraged by her confidante that she "blackens innocence" to commit the real crime of a slander ultimately homicidal—the crime she expiates at the end to the beloved's father, who is also her husband.

Not the passion itself is at work here, but the consequences of the passion as it bends back on itself. Love is visible to all eyes, and so the most careful concealments will vanish before the Argus-jealousy of a Mithridate or a Roxane. Hermione at the very moment of her presumptive triumph, shows in her one interview with Andromaque (III,4) that she is not, alas, in any way the dupe of her own forthcoming marriage.

The spurned lover knows within himself, by his own love, what the beloved's love for another implies. Those implications produce a powerful and irresistible outer logic of temporal event through the inner logic of their actions. Jealousy is not a static attribute, like power, or even like love itself. Since of its very nature it must feed on emptiness, it is condensed to the dynamism of wavering at the outside of love's steadfast-ness, even when the *jaloux* is one who, like Néron or Mithri-date, holds absolute power himself. As the underside of love, jealousy turns love against itself, moving towards a fulfillment that is doomed to a self-deprivation, with none of the resigned lover's transcendence. Because of jealousy's dynamic force the tragic presence of the third party, of Atalide in *Bajazet*, is not allowed to stay put with mere renunciation. The transport that brings the enraged Hermione to order a lover to murder her beloved is an amorous transport on both sides, compounded by jealousy on both sides. The dynamic of Oreste's love and jealousy leads him to illusion, then inevitably to disillusion. The dynamic of Hermione's leads her to the illusion of self-assertion which is really self-deprivation, and then to self-immolation. So Phèdre's dynamic, leading her presumably to the self-concealment of shame, really leads her in her jealous lack of peace to the self-revelation of her honorable suicide. Love alone, in its all-powerful and honorable simplicity, would merely assert its plenum at the point of its eclipse:

J'aime assez mon amant pour renoncer à lui

says Atalide in *Bajazet* (III,1), as all the characters of *Bérénice*, too, would say—at the final moment of recognized honor. Just before that moment Bérénice had shown a rage recognizably akin to that of Phèdre, Roxane, Mithridate, and Hermione; Titus and Antiochus had each spoken of the suicide she too had been planning. To come back round to a love-in-renunciation allows Antiochus also to share in the transcendence, to get beyond the effects of jealousy.

Love takes one out of oneself in a "transport." The natural condition of man is a trans-natural one, and the overriding motive in a society presumably subdued to political organization is the profoundly personal one that willingly crosses political allegiances to attain its ends. The *transport* is a *destin*, to take as equivalent the two words used in different drafts of one line of *Andromaque*,[42] and also the transport is something stronger than a destiny, since for

Je me livre en aveugle au destin qui m'entraine.

I give myself blindly, to the fate that draws me.

Racine had substituted in the later editions:

Je me livre en aveugle au transport qui m'entraine.

(I,1)

Some lesser personage totally devoted to politics, the Acomat of *Bajazet*, can brush aside at one stroke (IV,7) the amorous design we have been presuming him to hold through the play; we have proceeded on the assumption that a suitor is transcendentally amorous till proven otherwise. Pyrrhus betrays all political considerations, his loyalty to the Greeks, and his own military nature, to court and then marry an enemy, while Phèdre and Hippolyte, so different in other respects, resemble one another in their willingness to forget their political interests over the suppositious succession to Thésée, in favor of pursuing their amorous designs. Hippolyte will share an empire with the sister of his enemies as readily as Phèdre will sacrifice the rights of her own children to the proposed realization of her love. She will become quasi-legitimate, or at least casuistically justifiable (I,5), once the "death" of her husband releases her to entertain as a suitor his own son by a different mother.

It is in the context of a political intrigue over succession that we have seen these courtship confrontations. Hippolyte denies his love to Aricie at first (I,1). But at the news of his father's death he pays her a visit, ostensibly only to free her from Thésée's ban against marrying, but actually, as it soon appears, to propose himself, and to resign half his power in her favor. He had underestimated the overpowering effect of her presence (II,2). Just so, before he leaves the stage, is he confronted by Phèdre, who offers the same power-sacrifice to him. For her he creates a frustration that will bring about their mutual downfall, annulling the fulfillment seemingly promised him in the prior scene. The imperial power, of Thésée or Mithridate, Pyrrhus or Roxane, simply gives leverage to the open love of its possessor.

The imperial challenge, of Rome's opposition or the father's priority in *Mithridate*, of the lovers' imprisonment in *Bajazet*, heightens the love in the natural course of the action, simply because the lovers must display their affection in the process of coming to terms with the dominant problem. Imperial force also steeps the tragedy with a sense that there is a strong need for the refuge of love in the allopathic contagion of despair over the limitations of power. In the wilderness of all these checks and balances, one shared Eden presents itself to the open heart, and nearly all hearts are open. Britannicus and

Junie have grown up in the shadow of palace terror; he has
been eased out of imperial succession, while her brother has
been murdered. They have sought each other out as the one
possible island of consoling trust.

The political intrigue, even when in *Mithridate* and *Bérénice*
it involves both halves of the known world, serves at best as
a pretext for the profound currents that are carrying it along.
It doesn't matter, in the face of his silent love for Atalide, that
Bajazet is willing to save his life by going along with the desperate declaration of Roxane:

> *Songez-vous que je tiens les portes du Palais,*
> *Que je puis vous ouvrir ou fermer pour jamais,*
> *Que j'ai sur votre vie un empire suprême...*
> *Et sans ce même amour, qu'offensent vos refus,*
> *Songez-vous, en un mot, que vous ne seriez plus?*
>
> (II,1)

> Do you realize that I hold the palace gates,
> That I can open or close them for you forever,
> That I hold supreme sway over your life...
> And without this love that your refusals offend,
> Do you realize, in a word, that you would be no more?

Bajazet agrees, expands her word "empire" to "gloire" and
reinterprets it in the changed sense that capitalization indicates;
but in his scrupulous fidelity to the woman he really loves, he
avoids so much as touching on the word "amour":

> *Oui, je tiens tout de vous; et j'avais lieu de croire*
> *Que c'était pour vous-même une assez grande gloire,*
> *En voyant devant moi tout l'Empire à genoux,*
> *De m'entendre avouer que je tiens tout de vous.*
>
> (II,1)

> Yes, I hold all from you; I had grounds to think
> That for yourself it was glory great enough,

In seeing before me the Empire is on its knees,
To hear me vouch that I hold all from you.

Avouer and *tout* are feints: but of course no declaration other than an amorous one can satisfy, nor can the rage of Roxane ever harness its absolute authority to find any peace.

Oreste, again, arrives with the announced mission of facing Pyrrhus as an emissary of the Greeks; he is to transmit a political order to one of their kings. Neither is deceived for a moment from realizing that the mainspring of their encounter is that of an unsuccessful rival before a successful but indifferent one. The labyrinth of pretexts has only one issue: *Empire, gloire,* and all the great honorific values of public life, to which Racine simply subscribed and which formed the substance of his audience's public code, here act as preliminaries of one internal finality. Duty merely expands love. In the political sphere Racine is fully Cornelian; it is true, as Bénichou says for Corneille, that Racine exhibits an opposition between "l'orgueil et la force."[43] And it is also true, as for Corneille, that "ce qu'il cherche, c'est un accord où l'orgueil lui même autorise la loi, où les limitations que la société... rend indispensables, se confondent avec les intérèts de la gloire." But he never allows this complexity a triumphant idealization or a final resolution. Even an underling like Panope knows that a complex summary of a political situation offers only an illusory preoccupation:

Pour le choix d'un maître Athènes se partage.
Au Prince votre fils l'un donne son suffrage,
Madame, et de l'Etat l'autre oubliant les lois,
Au fils de l'étrangère ose donner sa voix.
On dit même qu'au trône une brigue insolente
Veut placer Aricie et le sang de Pallante.
J'ai cru de ce péril vous devoir avertir.
Déjà même Hippolyte est tout prêt à partir;
Et l'on craint, s'il paraît dans ce nouvel orage,
Qu'il n'entraîne après lui tout un peuple volage.

(I,4)

Athens divides on the choice of master.
One party gives its vote to the Prince, your son,
Lady, and the other, forgetting the State's laws,
Dares give its voice to the stranger's son.
It is said one insolent cabal even wants
To put Aricie and Pallante's blood on the throne.
I thought I ought to warn you of this danger.
Even now Hippolyte is ready to depart,
And it is feared if he appears in this new storm
He will drag after him the whole fickle populace.

In a similar fashion does Panope brief the distracted Phèdre immediately upon the announcement of Thésée's death, in words carrying strong ironic overtones about the dominant situation, the erotic one. For all her brevity, she has gone on too long, and Oenone, before Phèdre's own silence, disposes of it herself:

Panope, c'est assez. La Reine, qui t'entend,
Ne négligera point cet avis important.
(I,4)

Panope, it's enough. The Queen, who awaits you,
Will not neglect this important message.

No *avis*, no message about third parties, can be as important as the *avoue*, the confession of love in the intimacy of a couple, which Hippolyte will now go forth to make to Aricie, on the heels of this same news.

Beside the final truth, everything else has the status of a lie. When Thésée returns, the political intrigue, in all its temporariness, vanishes, and he is abused by the big lie of Hippolyte's infidelity, before which he will not believe the more modest and more profound truth ("La fille de Pallante a vaincu votre fils") of his son's love for an enemy's daughter ("Tu te feins criminel pour te justifier" [IV,4]). While the all-important condemnation of the stepson she loves is being mounted, Phèdre, with the unerring instinct of a lover, can react only to the truth of this particular news ("Oenone, qui l'eût cru? j'avais une rivale.").

In *Iphigénie* alone, a secularized religious purpose, a primitive and horrifying one, balances against a marriage through all the play's intricacy of purpose and feints towards solution. As the action progresses, when the Sacrifice is in, the Marriage is out. The same girl seems to be moving inexorably to the same altar, where at the last moment either ceremony could be performed, and both cannot be, over the same girl. But both are; the secret truth declares all the impelling actions and counteractions to have been a preliminary error. The issue of Eriphile's own passion can only be to immolate herself, to accomplish the destiny she has been magnetized towards as she seeks out Calchas; since, when her passion is not reciprocated, she may as well die. Her real, hidden name is also Iphigénie. Still, she is fixed wholly on her suicidal self-sacrifice. To the last she conceals in herself the element of jealous despair underlying her action, nor in her own account (IV,3) is there any mention of the inevitable happiness of the rival-homonymous double, with whom, in her one vocal encounter, she has fatally argued (II,5). The sacrifice neutralizes all other actions, and still the last words are of a marriage for which Ulysse's statesmanly definition, *auguste alliance*, is as inadequate as Clytemnestre's final *bienfaits* is imprecise. Under the shadow of those *bienfaits*, the last word of the play, the lovers are to move out into joys which have nothing to do with the sacrifice that has stopped their delineation but not their existence.

The power that is present, on stage, in the theatre, is the power of love. All past powers set the stage, as the past for the present. If the future is cut off, the love will still be eternal, as Phèdre knows:

OENONE
Quel fruit recevront-ils de leurs vaines amours?
Ils ne se verront plus.

OENONE
What fruit will they receive from their vain loves?
They will see one another no more.

To which Phèdre replies—and it says everything of this world:

Ils s'aimeront toujours.

(IV,6)

They will always love.

The dimensions of a future is not essential to this love, and it can make itself present out of any combination from the past.

In the extreme civilization of Racine's language, in the mannered political awareness of their gestures, these characters are unmythologically subjected to the power that lies in all myth. Not myth but the effect of myth, the envisioned love invests the language of enactment and provides a sympathetic structure wherein what is apprehended, the *compassion*, overcomes what is feared, the *terreur*.

Its presentness of power idealizes the love as well as abstracting it. In whatever condition of loss, Racine lays bare on stage a passion not only of inevitable primacy, but of ineluctable desirability. Whatever else may be desirable, love stands as more so, in the presentness of its power, before all pasts and futures. The bare unified stage submits to and unifies the absolute power of the state and the ultimate power of love in a single "lieu stupéfié," to adapt Barthes' phrase about the Racinian space.[44] The love whose ambivalence in Racine's society has been shorn away and laid bare to a single, unde-

niable profound motive, and the empire that has been taken
at its full face value and simply compounded against the love—
these two ingredients, not only different in themselves but
adopted differently from the context of the actual scene of
his time—come together in an iron equivalence of time and
space to direct the movement of the play forward.

These ironed-out components of the stage plenum intensify
the slacker, but more complex, real life outside the door of the
theater. In that real life Racine can console himself after the
death of Du Parc with la Champmeslé, and then go on to a
happy marriage of convenience; Louis XIV can weep over
Marie Mancini but go on to others, and then to Madame de
Maintenon. For Titus and Pyrrhus, Atalide and Phèdre, Xipharès
and Junie, there are no others. The closed stage eternalizes
the maximum possibility for those actualities. What is tragic
is also ideal; the *compassion* embraces the self as well as the
other. In doing so it embraces the self of the spectator as well as
the other on the speaking stage: the paradigm of the stage-
language is resolved and intensified through enacting the most
intensified form of two-way language, the love that by the
very act of seeking fulfillment can triumphantly speak the
presence of its power.

Chapter Six

THE POWER OF ENACTMENT:
CORNEILLE

1

Racine makes his characters display their reciprocities so urgently that the process of trying to achieve fulfillment carries them beyond it. This process is rendered even more urgent because the reciprocities depend deeply on a sentiment that is deeply opposed to display, the intimate inclination of erotic attachment, something at once transparent to the beholder and forbidden to all eyes but those of the lover. Concordantly, in the syntax of the alexandrines that serve the characters as the vehicle of expression, he intensifies the balances of a recitative convention, whose essence is display, in order to transcend it. In a form where the relation of language to action is that of manifest content to manifest content,[45] he has the displaying recitative of the language undermine itself to transcend itself, by giving the recitative a drift that follows the contours of the speaker's latent content, his struggles to manage an all-powerful love. In the connection of what someone recites to the way he recites point for point, in the congruence of an entire speech, we hear either a relatively vacillating disturbance of the soul or a relatively firm self-mastery. Over a whole speech both firmness and vacillation transpire through the uniformly controlled little-plenums of its paired and balanced parts. It is not just in the separate turns of phrase that we are given "klassische Dämpfung," a muting effect of classical style, to adapt Leo Spitzer's term for the process by which "an emotional stream of narrative is interrupted by intellectual evaluations"[46] in the "continuous representation of the emotional by the intellectual."[47] Such "intellectual" phrases as "digne fils d'un héros", in the messenger's speech of Théramène about Hippolyte's death (to take Spitzer's cited example), carry the emotion not just in themselves, but as they are coordinated by the drift of one statement's connection with another. Even here in the speech of someone unsubjected to the dramatized passions, the "emotional" message is not just interrupted by intellectual definitions; the speech is intellectual at every single point and the emotion shows through most triumphantly in the eruptive drift of the speaker from point to point as his emotion prevents him from maintaining intellectual control. And the force of emotion, in the spectators of the audience who respond to the force of this spectator on stage, derives from what we have already seen: in this example, from the actions that make Hippolyte *digne*. This speech wrings for sorrowful ironic response our sense of how truly he is a *fils* whom the *héros* has not yet come to see as such.

The alexandrine itself, as an unvarying abstract pattern, constitutes a "klassische Dämpfung".

Corneille, whose "static" quality Cassirer and others have contrasted with the "dynamic" quality of Racine,[48] contains his recitative even more fully in the pattern he gloriously tautened. Corneille's speeches do confine, couplet by couplet, the plenum of emotion to the manifest recitation of its possible logical contrasts. For example, when Auguste in *Cinna* goes through his first battle with himself over whether to punish the conspirators or pardon them, he states one entire argument *con*, and then changes over, in the other half of a couplet, to the argument *pro*, pivoting on the one logical word *Mais*:

> *Punissons l'assassin, proscrivons les complices.*
> *Mais quoi? toujours du sang, et toujours des supplices!*
>
> (IV,2)

> Let's punish the assassin, proscribe the accomplices.
> But what? Forever blood, forever tortures!

And once he has stated it, he stays firmly with the prevailing alternative in a way that the inwardness of Racine's characters never permits them. Within each line, too, *assassin* balances *complices*, and *sang* balances *supplices*. When they are agitated, Corneille's characters do not, as Racine's do, manifest by logical drift their internal subjection to powerful contradictory forces. Rather, they recite the uniform contrasts. So the Félix of *Polyeucte* retains his logical balance of speech even in the midst of that very confusion which becomes his imperfect but sufficient motive (he is not motiveless, as some commentators claim) for conversion to Christianity:

> *On ne sait pas les maux dont mon coeur est atteint:*
> *De pensers sur pensers mon âme est agitée,*
> *De soucis sur soucis elle est inquiétée;*
> *Je sens l'amour, la haine, et la crainte, et l'espoir,*
> *La joie et la douleur tour à tour l'emouvoir;*
> *J'entre en des sentiments qui ne sont pas croyables:*
> *J'en ai de violents, j'en ai de pitoyables,*
> *J'en ai de généreux qui n'oseraient agir,*
> *J'en ai même de bas, et qui me font rougir.*
>
> (III,5)

> Is is not known what ills attack my heart:
> With thought after thought my soul is agitated,
> With care after care it is disquieted;
> I feel love, and hate, and fear, and hope,
> Joy and sorrow move me each in turn;
> I enter on feelings that are not believable.
> I have violent ones, have pitiable ones,
> Have magnanimous ones that don't dare act,
> And even have base ones that make me blush.

Here, where all is recitative naming of emotions, all the names are balances. What is vacillation in Racine, here goes only as far as balanced attribution. One line balances another, one

half-line contrasts its second half, and we know where we are
going, in a sense, all the time: we can rest confidently on the
assumption that one logical half of conclusion will complement
its half of logical premise, even within the single line, for every
single line.

Racine takes this expectation—that the second half of an
alexandrine will balance the first, or the second line of a couplet
close out the first—and transforms it utterly: he disappoints
the expectation (his sense of loss) by a tremendous simplicity
(his sense of plenum). Instead of "j'en ai de violents" being
expectedly followed by "j'en ai de pitoyables," he allows his
second term to go almost anywhere after his first.

It is against the disappointed expectation of such comple-
mentarity that certain lines and couplets, appearing on the face
of it to be merely narrative, gain their surprising enacted power:

> Dans l'Orient désert—quel devint mon ennui.

> In the desert East what did my boredom become.

The sense of *ennui* is created not only in the condensation of
the individual words, and not only in the various connections
in the logic of the line,[49] but also in the fact that "l'Orient
désert" is *not* balanced.

In

> Ariane ma soeur! de quel amour blessée
> Vous mourûtes aux bords où vous fûtes laissée!

> Ariadne, my sister, wounded with what love
> Did you die on the shores where you were abandoned!

there is an important disappointment over and above the
balance of the second line. The balances themselves are complex:
mourûtes equals *fûtes* since both are past; but contrasts with
it since one is an auxiliary and the other is a full verb form,

since "dying" is the opposite of "existing", and since "laissée"—we learn with the last word that "fûtes" was not after
all another full verb form—itself stands to *mourûtes* as lesser
ill to greater, as cause to effect. In the language the time order
is reversed, *mourûtes*, the effect, coming before *fûtes laissée*,
the cause. Still, even more predominantly than all these balances,
themselves so shifting that they hint at their own subversion,
this couplet moves its sigh in the main movement from the
first half of a line to the last half, through a prevailing lack of
balance between "soeur" and "de quel amour blessée," and
between "bords" and "laissée." Further, the narrative of a
sorrowful end, carried in the simple movement from "blessée"
to "mourûtes," strongly overrides the couplet break and disappoints any rhythmic sense of applicable summary. Indeed,
those who are wounded do sometimes die. It will happen so
to the speaking heroine herself. In this single couplet Phèdre is
struggling to conceal; she is answering, and agreeing to, and
rejecting, Oenone's immediately preceding injunction that for
all the future "un silence éternel cache ce souvenir." Here,
then, is still another *souvenir* than that of her mother, closer to
home in many ways, and still quite distant from the suffering
woman we see on stage. The "disappointed" balances of the
verse give voice to these other multiple, and ultimately mortal,
sighs of disappointment.

  The Racinian movement against the full exploitation by which
Corneille had dramatized the balanced language of the couplet
gives the speaker the advantage of suggesting greater fulfillment
by opening the expected balance wider. At the same time, by
refraining from couplet balance, Racine dramatizes the loss
from a plenum; the failure to attain completeness is "audible"
in the very form he is using. This supple power at deflecting
expected balances, provides overtones for the briefest utterances.
At the same time it orchestrates the long speeches magnificently. So Phèdre's declaration to Hippolyte moves tangenti-
ally from an initial comparison—as always not permitting the
neat completeness of full couplet balance—between the son and
the father. She begins, too, not with a contrast but with the

capping amplification of an agreement that it is Thésée she
longs for: "Toujours de son amour votre âme est embrasée,"
(II,5), Hippolyte has said. His own line amplifies instead of
balancing, full as he comes to her himself with his freshly
declared love for Aricie. She is also a secret lover, and she
replies:

> Oui, Prince, je languis, je brûle pour Thésée.
> Je l'aime, non point tel que l'ont vu les enfers,
> Volage adorateur de mille objets divers,
> Qui va du Dieu des morts déshonorer la couche;
> Mais fidèle, mais fier, et même un peu farouche,
> Charmant, jeune, traînant tous les coeurs après soi,
> Tel qu'on dépeint nos Dieux, ou tel que je vous voi.
> Il avait votre port, vos yeux, votre langage,
> Cette noble pudeur colorait son visage,
> Lorsque de notre Crète il traversa les flots,
> Digne sujet des Voeux des filles de Minos.
> Que faisiez-vous alors? Pourquoi sans Hippolyte
> Des héros de la Grèce assembla-t-il l'élite?
> Pourquoi, trop jeune encor, ne pûtes-vous alors
> Entrer dans le vaisseau qui le mit sur nos bords?
> Par vous aurait péri le monstre de la Crète,
> Malgré tous les détours de sa vaste retraite.
> Pour en développer l'embarras incertain,
> Ma soeur du fil fatal eût armé votre main.
> Mais non, dans ce dessein je l'aurais devancée:
> L'amour m'en eût d'abord inspiré la pensée.
> C'est moi, Prince, c'est moi dont l'utile secours
> Vous eût du Labyrinthe enseigné les détours.
> Que de soins m'eût coûtés cette tête charmante!
> Un fil n'eût point assez rassuré votre amante.
> Compagne du péril qu'il vous fallait chercher,
> Moi-même devant vous j'aurais voulu marcher;
> Et Phèdre au Labyrinthe avec vous descendue
> Se serait avec vous retrouvée, ou perdue.

(II,5)

Yes, Prince, I languish, I burn for Thésée.
I love him, not as the underworld has seen him,
Fickle adorer of a thousand diverse objects,
Who was to stain the couch of the God of the dead;
But faithful, proud, and even a little wild,
Charming, young, drawing all hearts after him,
As they portray our Gods, or as I look at you.
He had your bearing, your eyes, your language,
That noble modesty colored his face,
When he traversed the floods of our Crete,
Worthy subject for the vows of Minos' daughters.
What did you do then? How without Hippolyte
Did he gather the elite of Greece's heroes?
Why, still too young, did you not enter then
The vessel that set him down upon our shores?
At your hands the Cretan monster would have perished
For all the byways of his vast retreat.
To open out the chancy perplexity,
My sister would have armed your hand with the fatal
  thread.
No—I would have been ahead of her in this purpose:
Love would have first inspired that thought in me.
It is I, Prince, it is I whose useful help
Would have taught you the byways of the Labyrinth.
What cares this charming head would have cost me!
A thread would not have assured your lover enough.
Companion of that danger you had to seek,
I myself would have wanted to walk in front of you,
And Phèdre, gone down with you to the Labyrinth,
Would with you have been found out, or lost.

The internal power of Phèdre's passion is here enacted in
the logical lapses from one half line to another, of her failure
to provide syntactic balance, and in the rhythmical dispropor-
tions of her managing the proportionate form, from the very
second line, where *je l'aime* cannot help simply continuing the

asyndeton of *je languis, je brûle*. The emphasis of *non point*, which seems to be contrasting the old Thésée with the more desireable young one, drops its mask in the process of heaping up the six adjectival terms, two qualified by *mais* and the other four again in the slur of asyndeton. All this pretense at logic is subverted by the seeming afterthought-alternative of "ou tel que je vous voi."

At once a fantasy narrative overrides the mere balanced comparison of attributes "Why weren't you there?" "If you had been, my sister Ariadne (the *de quel amour, blessée* of earlier!) would have helped you." "Or no, I would have helped you." "I wouldn't just have given you a thread, I'd have gone into the labyrinth myself." Under the power of this suggestion upon the speaker, all her logical balances are lost in the simple account, until she has reached the conclusion, and restored the imagined balance—the sole line of the speech that contains such a clear contrast—of the equally fantasied alternatives of the last two participles, where the logical antithesis between *retrouvée* and *perdue* is undermined by their identity as erotic fulfillment for Phèdre, and still more by their status as shocking revelation for Hippolyte, a terrible complication for the audience. Manifestly the speech began as a logical summary of her devotion to her husband. The lack of the connection which the speech "should have" been supporting produces here the enacted sense of the one big latent connection she is declaring in spite of herself, drawn into it by the very obsessiveness of the passion. One line may manage the passion, but a whole speech cannot— just as Pyrrhus may be resolute or Hermione may be vindictive in a single gesture but may not hold to one such counter-erotic course through the entire series of an action.

Corneille's triumph is to accept the balance of his line as a given, and to recite through that. (Perhaps Racine's "failure" to do so led the older man, at the height of his fame, to declare that the younger had no talent for drama.) Chimène's climactic declaration to Rodrigue, for all her strain, holds to the power of the dialectical balances in which she is wholly trammelled.

Rodrigue himself has finished by announcing, in balanced
couplets as always, that in the duel against Don Sanche's
defense of her father's murder, he will let himself be killed by
his opponent because he is her champion:

> *Je vais lui présenter mon estomac ouvert,*
> *Adorant en sa main la vôtre que me perd.*
>
> (V,1)

The last line caps the contrast between *sa main* and *la vôtre*;
so, too, in the glorious reaches of honor, between *adorant*
and *me perd*. Chimène begins by a logical conversion of these
terms into *juste* versus *triste* and *devoir* versus *violence*:

> *Si d'un triste devoir la juste violence,*
> *Qui me fait malgré moi poursuivre ta vaillance,*
> *Prescrit à ton amour une si forte loi*
> *Qu'il te rend sans défense à qui combat pour moi,*
> *En cet aveuglement ne perds pas la mémoire*
> *Qu'ainsi que de ta vie il y va de ta gloire,*
> *Et que dans quelque éclat que Rodrigue ait vécu,*
> *Quand on le saura mort, on le croira vaincu.*
> *Ton honneur t'est plus cher que je ne te suis chère,*
> *Puisqu'il trempe tes mains dans le sang de mon père,*
> *Et te fait renoncer, malgré ta passion,*
> *A l'espoir le plus doux de ma possession.*
>
> (V,1)

If a sad duty's just violence,
Which makes me in spite of myself pursue your valor
Prescribes for your love a law so strong
That it puts you defenseless against who fights for me,
In this blindness do not lose the memory
That your life is in question as well as your glory,
And that in whatever brilliance Rodrigue has lived,

When he is known to be dead, he will be thought over-
come.
Your honor is dearer to you than I am,
Since it dips your hands in the blood of my father,
And makes you renounce, in spite of your passion,
The most tender hope of possessing me.

There is not a line, a hemistich, or a larger verse paragraph
here that does not have its major logical balance. The constant
sense of alternatives, each of which is an absolute, tautens
the language into an equivalent of the iron pradoxes which are
so demanding that the character can never account for them:
all this talk merely keeps setting them out. The talk, as a
whole, testifies to the courage and honor which by continuing
to face the paradoxes, will work them through to an enacted
conclusion. No one falters, and the occasion for faltering
presents itself in the linkage of every alternative, at the caesura
of every line. The power to transcend the logic is manifested
in the consistency with which the full force of the logic is
maintained at every moment.

In Racine the tight relations converge upon the single faulty
link toward which the breaks in the logic of the verse are then
forever leaking away; in Corneille the loyalties divided within
the mind and heart of the character stand at a draw, and the
sustained balance of the verse keeps them at that point of
draw until the whole course of the action can relieve them.[50]
Both writers, in their opposite ways, face the poetic obligation
of heroic coherence and extreme pressure; both, interestingly,
had similar methods of composition, if we are to believe Louis
Racine's account of his father's practices;[51] and both writers
would seem to have planned for their plays an austere pro-
portionateness. As May points out,[52] Thésée's return in *Phèdre*
is announced at verse 828 of a tragedy that has 1,654: at the
exact beginning of the second half; and as early as *La Suivante*,[53]
Corneille saw to it that each of his scenes had exactly 340

verses. Their radically different uses of the *parole dramatique*, in which Racine pitches all on the passionate response and Corneille on the public declaration of control, derive from a comparable concern for the presentation of an elemental coherence. This coherence appears in the language, as much as it does in the unities of time, place, and action. That first and last of the unities in literature, unity of language, is served by the merely Aristotelian ones.

2

Before Corneille reached, in the *Cid*, the point at which he could oppose perplexed love not to some erotic alternative but to a value equally imposing, that of family loyalty, he had to work his way through seven other plays. In each of the six comedies he tried to treat an amorous problem, one which in the *Examens* he wrote towards the end of his career he is at pains to specify as a particular sphere for each. That specialization, helped by his refocussing away from the pastoral tradition onto a measured realism,[54] brought him only towards the limited mastery of *La Suivante*. Moreover, the negative absolutism of Alidor in *La Place Royale* finds no countervailing value. The dramatic inventiveness already apparent in the *Cymbeline*-like variety of his second play, *Clitandre*, and still manifest in the prison scene of *Médée* (a detail he criticizes in his *Examen* of that play) had also to be sacrificed. And so, apparently for one test play, did the Catholic universe: *Médée* is the first play in which the characters do not share the devotional loyalties of the author, and the first play whose plot he did not invent himself. Still, he works through a strangely metatheatrical fantasy in *L'Illusion*, with its spectator-setting reminiscent of the *Taming of the Shrew*, before purifying at last in the *Cid* the tensions that will stay with his theatre to the end. There, too, though the persons are Catholic, he has revised religiosity out of a still more Catholic original; and the *Cid* differs notably from its source in cutting out the religious effusions.[55] The sublimity of his lovers there is worked out wholly on the ground of their response and responsiveness to the conflicting ideals they cannot defect from without self-violation and seemingly cannot reconcile without self-contradiction.

"Chez lui," Cassirer says, "tout est comme accordé à un seul ton; à la force et à la durée de résonance."[56] The "buckle" in Rousset's schematism of his plots, does not become a "drill" of spiralling self-transcendence until the last act.[57] In a sense, too, all that is revealed, "statically", is the fundament of nobility holding the action from the beginning. The "drill" only reveals a perfect "buckle."

The character's sense of himself, a sort of *cogito* in Cassirer's reading,[58] does not, either in thought or in will, bring him to the unity that only the worked-out action can achieve: or, as Serge Doubrovsky puts it, "Le projet aristocratique...s'oppose fondamentalement au projet stoïque, en ce qu'il réclame et suscite la présence d'un autre à qui se montrer supérieur."[59] Corneille does participate in as well as transcend the Stoic revival of his time, and his personages are never involved in showing themselves as superior to anything but their own worst instincts. They resemble Racine's in the profound equality of their humanity.

In the *Cid*, as though to insist on the identity of the human lot, there is for each protagonist a corresponding figure in both love and duty, Don Sanche for Chimène and the Infante for Rodrigue. The Infante exhibits her magnanimity not only in overlooking the rank her duty obliges her to keep in view, but also in her austere silence about her love, and finally in handing over Rodrigue to Chimène (V,7):

Sèche tes pleurs, Chimène, et reçois sans tristesse
Ce généreux vainqueur des mains de ta princesse.

Dry your tears, Chimène, and receive without sadness
This magnanimous victor from the hands of your prin-
    cess.

Don Sanche shows his magnanimity not only in his willingness to incur the same probable death in facing Rodrigue that
the young Rodrigue had faced before Chimène's father, not
only in risking the fate, so to speak, of Racine's Oreste by
going out to kill her beloved (a possibility that materializes
in the illusion of Act 5, Scene 5), but also by stepping forth
generously to add his felicitations to them in his renunciatory
praise of an *amour parfait*.

The absoluteness to which Corneille's major characters are
subjected, the total power under which and towards which
they enact, derives not from obstacles to overmastering passion—
they may be found even in the renunciation of *La Place Royale*
or in the self-denial of *La Veuve*—but rather in the equal status
between the obstacle and the love (an absoluteness that may
have led Corneille to change the designation of the Cid as
Doubrovsky notes, from *tragi-comédie* to *tragédie*[60]). That absoluteness finds its embodiment in the person who presides over
the society's ideals: in the king. And yet it is to stand wholly
outside the universe of Corneille's theatre—it is to cease to
become the spectator of his play—to insist with Leo Lowenthal
on the arbitrary character of the king's sway,[61] or even with
Doubrovsky on the essential value of sustaining the monarchic
order.[62]

In the play itself, the monarchic order, as the king speaks,
is only the dimension in militarily maintained space (as parent-
hood is in honored time) of a central nobility of soul to which,
through Don Rodrigue and Chimène (as also through everyone
else, notably Don Sanche and the Infante), both the *amour*
and the *devoir* are doing homage in the act of proving their
existence. *Al cor gentil ripara sempre amore*: it requires nobility
to love, and nobility tends to love. Guinizelli's formula is here,

so to speak, enacted. It is, indeed, just because the lovers insist at every point in following both *devoir* and *amour* that the conflict between the two ideals is resolved as the ground common to both is laid bare in the action.

If at the beginning Don Rodrigue had insisted on his father's share of fault in the impulsive quarrel he is asked to revenge, he should not have challenged his future father-in-law to a duel. (Or if his father had heeded the king's injunction to stop; "Qu'aux volontés du Roi ce grand courage cède." [II,1]) Or if he had listened (as the Comte admits he could not in honor do) to the highly persuasive speech of the Comte that for all of them the best course would be to forget about the duel (II,2), he might have married Chimène and worked out the complications with his father on the level of diplomacy and prudence. Chimène herself, for all the mortal danger involved, sees her lover's dilemma clearly and expresses it to the Princesse she does not know also loves him:

> S'il ne m'obéit point, quel comble à mon ennui!
> Et s'il peut m'obéir, que dira-t-on de lui?
>
> (II,3)

> If he obeys me not, what a peak to my annoyance!
> And if he can obey, what will they say of him?

Through the whole center of the play they strain against, and test, their impasse. She must demand death for the beloved who has killed her father (II,8), and he must respond (III,4) by offering her the very sword to kill him. The logic tightens as the emotion tightens. But the nobility (the word *digne* covers *amour* and *devoir*) is still expressly the single definer:

> Tu t'es, en m'offensant, montré digne de moi;
> Je me dois, par ta mort, me montrer digne de toi.
>
> (III,4)

In offending me you have shown yourself worthy of me;
I must, by your death, show myself worthy of you.

If, at the end, he had gone through with the duel towards
Don Sanche, he might also have married her, and she would
have been content; she urges him to this course in so many
words:

Et si tu sens pour moi ton coeur encore épris,
Sors vainqueur d'un combat dont Chimène est le prix.
(V,1)

And if you feel your heart still to be won for me,
Be victor in a combat whose prize is Chimène.

But in addition to the spoken reservation—his love forbids his
lifting a sword against someone who is the champion of his
beloved—there is the reservation that his courtly reserve cannot
speak: he must make sure his beloved is delivered to him with
·her own nobility intact. Her nobility would suffer if he were
to win her by what would really be too easy a victory (and
not just a conjectured one, the Comte's earlier speculation)
over her champion. If Don Sanche's amorous ardor had been
sacrificed to Chimène's insistence on parental duty, then
Chimène would, not immediately but through a logic that the
action lays bare, have stood in bad faith; she would have solved
the impasse between *amour* and *devoir*, but at the cost of an
honor from which both those qualities derive. As Don Rodrigue,
the perfect suitor, lays bare this shadow of bad faith in her,
while at the same time humbled to the offered death before
her, she must resolve the question of honor before he is willing
to take her: before the *amour* is *parfait*, in Don Sanche's own
phrase. For her love to be perfect, she must suffer into good
faith both to have Rodrigue and for him to remain the man of
perfect honor. His love for her holds her not only to her duty
but to the logical consequences of her duty for her love. In

this sense, to the end, he fulfills Corneille's own description of him in the play's *Examen*, "Rodrigue suit ici son devoir sans rien relâcher de sa passion."

It is entirely, then, through their own interactive responses to each other's absolutisms, including the double take by-blow of Chimène's psychodramatically curative overanticipation in the false report of Rodrigue's death (V,5), that the lovers come together. The king's own impasse, by comparison, is merely administrative: how to fulfill Chimène's apparent demand to punish the Cid, and at the same time to reward the military leader who has defeated the Moors. The king gets out of his impasse by promising help to Chimène; and then, in the course of events, by waiting. He is there, however, to receive Chimène's declaration of love for her father's murderer (V,6), become honorable when the lover is "dead", and she requests that instead of marrying the victor she withdraw to the cloister. The role of the king here, it should be insisted, is never decisive. And at this point he merely reassures her that Don Rodrigue is alive, but also that her duty has been fulfilled.

> *Ta gloire est dégagée, et ton devoir est quitte;*
> *Ton père est satisfait, et c'était le venger*
> *Que mettre tant de fois ton Rodrigue en danger.*
> *Tu vois comme le ciel autrement en dispose.*

> Your glory is free and your duty has been paid;
> Your father is satisfied, and it avenged him
> To put your Rodrigue in danger so many times.
> You see how heaven has disposed otherwise.

What the king here attributes to "heaven" may be taken as an authoritative, but quite differently angled account of the process that has been enacted before our eyes. There is an element of providence or grace in the heroic adequacy of these two lovers to the logic of the seemingly mortal demands made

on them at every step. The events might have been different;
but given these events, they themselves rise to demonstrate an
underlying nobility.

The potentialities of the soul can only be known by the
grandeur it exhibits in extreme situations. Thus Corneille's
central dramatic talent (which it took him so long to disengage
from his subsidiary theatrical talent) displays tight extremities
towards the end of enacting that grandeur in an absolute,
untrammelled fullness. As Horace says in his own defense:

> Sire, c'est rarement qu'il s'offre une matière
> A montrer d'un grand coeur la vertu tout entière.
>
> (Horace, V,2)

> Sire, it is rarely there is offered a matter
> To display the entire virtue of a great heart.

The extreme balance of the Cid is raised to a more desperate
pitch in Horace, where the family, encompassing both the
love and the duty of the Cid, is set against a more abstract
obligation, the duty to the state. And that duty is presented
without any of the trappings of religiosity: it is not the Spanish
state, but the Roman.

In this play the pairings of equality are more symmetrical:
Horace the Roman is married to Sabine the Alban whose
brother Curiace is engaged to his sister Camille. That equality,
rigorously sustained, narrows down to a mortal, exemplary
combat of three Roman brothers against three Alban brothers—
one that will, by agreement, settle the mastery of the war for
their entire peoples. When, his two brothers killed, Horace alone
faces the three Alban brothers, Corneille carefully avoids
setting his ultimate in the merely physical situation: Horace,
as the illusion of his flight and Rome's defeat is reversed and
rectified, is recounted as having killed Curiace first (IV,2),
rather than last, the way the automatic suspense of the hack
playwright would infallibly have shown it. Since the least

wounded caught up with Horace first, Curiace would have shown himself thus as the most valorous survivor of the combat that killed Horace's two brothers. More consequential than the order of combat is the devotion to serve their people; on both sides "ces coeurs généreux n'y peuvent consentir" to the impulse of both armies to separate the enemy friends (III,2). And the paired women, as well as the men, must suffer the extremities from the beginning. Camille says so clearly:

> *Ce jour nous fut propice et funeste à la fois:*
> *Unissant nos maisons, il désunit nos rois;*
> *Un même instant conclut notre hymen et la guerre,*
> *Fit naître notre espoir et le jeta par terre,*
> *Nous ôta tout, sitôt qu'il nous eut tout promis,*
> *Et nous faisant amants, il nous fit ennemis.*
>
> (I,2)

> This day augured for us at once well and ill:
> Uniting our houses, it disunited our kings;
> One single instant sealed our marriage and the war,
> Made our hope be born and threw it to earth,
> Took all from us, once it had promised all,
> And making us lovers, made us enemies.

Still, Camille falters into accusation against the returning Horace over her Alban husband's death, and that vacillation is enough to make her brother kill her.

In the Roman context, Horace's impulsive action opens a new dimension: that of legality, and Corneille was a lawyer. He bends the question in the last act, when the king transcends legality not by delivering judgment but by asking the father, old Horace, to judge the young Horace. Sabine's gesture of magnanimity, to offer herself as the substitute for the husband who has killed her brother and countryman, puts her at a single stroke beyond the impasse of Chimène. What is central to the *Cid* has become in the pitch of this play only a subordinate possibility, the progress from her own version of Camille's rage in the request that her husband kill her too (IV,7) to her offer of herself as a sacrifice (V,3).

Old Horace's initial response had been to deplore the *honte* of the son's fratricide (rather than the death of his daughter [V,1]). When the king forces him to sit in judgment, he decides that Horace is *vertueux*. Tulle, as a king upholding the laws, can accept the judgment but not the definitions. Over what is past and not present the enactment has lost power, however, and the final word about Horace's excusing valor blames it only in principle:

> *Cette énorme action faite presque à nos yeux*
> *Outrage la nature, et blesse jusqu'aux Dieux.*
> *Un premier mouvement qui produit un tel crime*
> *Ne saurait lui servir d'excuse légitime:*
> *Les moins sévères lois en ce point sont d'accord;*
> *Et si nous les suivons, il est digne de mort.*
>
> (V,3)

> This enormous act almost in our eyes
> Does outrage to nature and wounds even the Gods.
> An initial movement producing such a crime
> Could not serve him as legitimate excuse:
> The least severe laws on this point are agreed;
> And if we follow them, he deserves death.

He goes on to weigh Horace's heroic service against his action, and to say that, as with Romulus, Rome can excuse the murder:

> *Elle peut bien souffrir en son libérateur*
> *Ce qu'elle a bien souffert en son premier auteur.*
> *Vis donc, Horace, vis, guerrier trop magnanime:*
> *Ta vertu met ta gloire au-dessus de ton crime;*

> She may well suffer in her liberator
> What she suffered so in the author of her being.

Live then, Horace, live, warrior of a spirit too great:
Your virtue puts your glory above your crime.

In this situation lies a contradiction, rather than an impasse to which any *vertu* could respond with resolution. Only a sacrifice can act to *purifier* it, and Tulle commands one. The pitch of the extremity, in the severity of the hero's exclusiveness, had carried him into a transgression of the very principle he was upholding, and the final admiration of the father offers no final word.

The power of the enactment here exceeds the power of its definition, whereas in the *Cid* both were adequate to one another. The lawyer's easy condemnation of Horace cedes to the dramatist's hard representation of his extreme situation. Not "to understand is to forgive," but "to admire is to reconcile."

Many such crimes lay on the path of the young Octave remembered in *Cinna*, most pronounced among them the proscription-execution of his old tutor, the father of Emilie. Having aged into the Auguste of the play, he does not blink his means to the throne, nor does anyone else in the play. In the face of those crimes he proves his transcendence of them by displaying magnanimity as a response to the treachery of conspiracy against his life. Cinna, chief conspirator, acting both for the honor of his family and for the love of the time-biding vengeful Emilie, has second thoughts before he is discovered; and Maxime, his co-conspirator and secret rival, goes through a whole series of betrayals against his friend and beloved as well as against his ruler. But under the magnetic example and encouragement of Auguste, all transcend themselves. Cinna accepts the sentence Auguste does not deliver, Maxime repents and publicly confesses; even Emilie, finally, yields to the emperor's unvarying magnanimity.

In Auguste's magnanimity we are given a startling insight into clemency as the last possibility of power, a feature that may have brought Stendhal to esteem Corneille so much beyond Racine. Nobility in political intrigue, displayed by all the

others intermittently and by Auguste steadily, is derived wholly
from the enacted gestures of the characters in response both
to the demands of the ideal and the demands of the power.
This enchainment of their authentic responsiveness saves the
play from the fatuous power-worship which the inattentive
modern spectator would be tempted to see in it. The empire
which had been a negative ideal in *Horace* is now made to yield
the utmost positive balance not only of personal nobility but
of governance.

In *Polyeucte*, Corneille, who in private life held parish
offices, returns to his Christianity via Rome. He convincingly
derives the aspirations of Christian sanctity from the positive
gestures of a comparable Roman nobility. The magnanimity—
the *générosité* to use Corneille's term—that enabled Auguste
to rule the Roman empire in *Cinna*, now brings one martyr
Néarque, and then his convert Polyeucte, into the realization
of a nobility transcending both love and the state. The *générosité* draws all into itself; Polyeucte ascribes Roman victories to
the Christian God, at the very point where he is publicly scorn-
ing the Roman gods (III,2). His wife, the *généreuse* Pauline,
facing the old lover whom her father had ordered her not to
marry, bravely indicates her abiding love while bidding him to
renounce in favor of her husband. Polyeucte, knowing her
heart, had generously left them alone. Thus she proves that
she equals, in that hardest sphere of Racinian natural erotic
inclination, her husband's transcendence of jealousy. Her constant management, and her later dutifulness to him in braving
the very father she had so desperately obeyed about Sévère,
already displays in her the process of producing on the "natural" level, within the sphere of the Roman family and state
as well as in the deeper realm of the heart, those gestures it
will take the logic of Corneille's invented action to render
Christian. Her conversion is implicit in her nobility, as her
father's conversion is implicit in the very principledness of his
puzzled vacillations: his bepuzzlement becomes adapted for
positive self-transcendence as he allows himself to enter the
faith without knowing exactly why:

Je m'y trouve forcé par un secret appas;
Je cède à des transports que je ne connais pas,
Et par un mouvement que je ne puis entendre,
De ma fureur je passe au zèle de mon gendre.

           (V,6)

I find myself forced by a secret appeal.
I cede to transports that I do not know,
And by a movement I cannot understand
From fury I pass to the zeal of my son-in-law.

In this absolute light, it is not necessary that Sévère marry Pauline, as Polyeucte has bidden the pair to do on the eve of his martyrdom. Nor is it necessary for Sévère to convert. He need only protect her, he need only state an admiration for the virtue of the Christians. In such enactment, his Roman virtue contains the possibility of conversion that is not even mentioned here, still less actualized. The circuit of possibility had already been closed in the martyrdoms and attendant conversions. Sévère had already demonstrated, in the natural nobility that offers the full ground of self-transcendence, his own equivalent capacity. The action defines him, and he needs no further definition; his loving honor fulfills him, and so it does not matter (what the sentimental audience wants to know) whether he gets this fulfillment. The "solidarité progressivement découverte," in Rousset's formulation, remains in progression. In this complex logic even his other formulation, "Il est vrai que la même conduite qui rapproche Pauline de Polyeucte éloigne Polyeucte de Pauline," works only on the level of erotic sympathy. Or as Rousset says: "La divergence n'est qu'apparente." All divergences, in the totality of the spirit that leads a noble person to diverge, issue in the actuality, or even the possibility only, of a grand convergence.

In these major plays, from the *Cid* through *Polyeucte*, almost no one is either evil or limited. A devotion to ultimate ideals gives each of the characters, even Maxime in *Cinna* and Félix in *Polyeucte*, the magic competence of rightness. But then, against such Romans in the later play *Pompée*, Corneille offers us a gallery of merely fearful and fraudulent, or merely powerful, Egyptians. There he conceals his noblest character of all; Pompée never appears, and the statements about him are reduced to Corneille's translations from Lucan.

Such evil, once envisaged, seems to free him to return to the sphere of the comedies and create, in *Le Menteur* and *La Suite du Menteur*, a *Cid*-like thoroughness of vision directed at the sort of mendacity that in the earlier comedies produces only miscellaneous effects and partial divergences. The style, too, is more transparent and slack, a reduction of Lope de Vega, as he says in his *Examen*. In the great, preceding trage- dies, he had been at pains to develop an appropriate stylistic vehicle for each turn of his extremes. In the *Cid*, it is the separate maxims that he speaks of as attracting the *auditeurs*, "des pensées brillantes dont il est semé"—though he is criti- cizing (backhandedly, because he is discussing his own defects) too exclusive an attention to those separable *pensées*. In *Horace* he finds in retrospect that his action had been too "moment- anée" (an attribution which holds also a sense of achievement: he had brought the pressure to bear on each contrastive moment). But he distinguishes both plays from *Cinna*:

> *Comme les vers d'*Horace *ont quelque chose de plus net et de moins guindé pour les pensées que ceux du* Cid, *on peut dire que ceux de cette pièce ont quelque chose de plus achevé. ...*

> As the verses of *Horace* have something neater and less forced for its thoughts than those of the *Cid*, one can say that those of this play have something in them more realized. ...

Actually, the verses of *Cinna* seem more *achevés* only in not being set to the service of the rending divergences felt at every moment of *Horace*: Corneille felt the positive idealism of

Cinna to transpire into the style. And he feels that when he has followed Minturnus, Heinsius, and Grotius (whom he cites in his *Examen*) to produce with *Polyeucte* a Christian version of Aristotle, the daring that sets a martyrdom on stage attains to the tenderness of devotion in the verses themselves:

> *Le style n'en est pas si fort ni si majestueux que celui de* Cinna *et de* Pompée, *mais il a quelque chose de plus touchant, et les tendresses de l'amour y font un agréable mélange avec la fermeté du divin.*

> Its style is neither so strong nor so majestic as that of *Cinna* or *Pompée*, but it has something more touching, and the tenderness of love mixes agreeably in it with the firmness of the divine.

It is at the same time the divine that he calls firm, the human tender, though in the success of their *mélange*, one could attribute either quality to each.

3

For Racine, to continue what Barthes rightly calls an inexhaustible comparison, the tenderness and the firmness are one internal quality, acknowledged in the prime response of two persons whose union is frustrated by some force embodied in a fatal third. For Corneille, on the other hand, the persons are always fully public as well as private. The contradictions work out in the open of the tight stage, and no one who is willing to meet the demands of heroic virtue, as nearly all are in the tragedies through *Polyeucte*, goes under to the condition of being a fatal third, or lapses in the sorrow of unifying tenderness and firmness. The abstract balances between *amour* and *devoir*, or between *famille* and *patrie*, or between *Dieu* and *empire*, can constantly skeletalize the poetry because they have done so in the full equivalences of the action.

The action of Corneille's plays, to use his own term, is *implexe*. And he is willing, almost like a modern writer, to attribute the failure of later works, including that of his favorite play, *Rodogune*, not to some wavering of his imagination (when all through the *Examens* he acknowledges his defects wholesale), but rather to the fatal inability of an audience to take more than one event at a time. The presentness of his - power, he asserts, is so great, that it pulls too many events into its unity and taxes the memory of the audience:

> *L'auditeur aime à s'abandonner à l'action présente, et à n'être point obligé, pour l'intelligence de ce qu'il voit, de réfléchir sur ce qu'il a déjà vu, et de fixer sa mémoire sur les premièrs actes, cependant que les derniers, sont devant ses yeux. C'est l'incommodité des pièces embarrassées, qu'en termes de l'art on nomme* implexes, *par un mot emprunté du latin, telles que sont* Rodogune *et* Heraclius. *Elle ne se rencontre pas dans les simples: mais comme celles-là ont sans doute besoin de plus d'esprit pour les imaginer, et de plus d'art pour les conduire, celles-ci, n'ayant pas le même secours du côté du sujet, demandent plus de force de vers, de raisonnement, et de sentiments pour les soutenir.*

The auditor likes to abandon himself to a present action and not to be obliged, so he may understand what he sees, to reflect on that which he has seen, and to fix his memory on the first acts when the last are before his eyes. That is the disadvantage of difficult plays, those called in the terms of the art "implex", a word borrowed from Latin—plays like *Rodogune* and *Heraclius*. It is not met in simple ones: but the former must doubtless have more wit to be imagined, and more art to carry them out; the latter, not getting the same help from subject matter, demand more force in the verse, a reasoning and sentiments to sustain them.

THE POWER OF ENACTMENT

Here at the end he is going a long way towards admitting a
lack of force to the poetry of *Rodogune* in the course of
explaining what has been called for to lend force to that of
Cinna.

For *Rodogune* itself, he wants to ascribe his preference to
the mounting progression of the action—though he has for-
gotten his qualification above to claim for it, among all its
other attributes, *la force des vers* as well:

> *Elle a tout ensemble la beauté du sujet, la nouveauté*
> *des fictions, la force des vers, la facilité de l'expression,*
> *la solidité du raisonnement, la chaleur des passions,*
> *les tendresses de l'amour et de l'amitié; et cet heureux*
> *assemblage est ménagé de sorte qu'elle s'élève d'acte*
> *en acte. Le second passe le premier, le troisième est*
> *au-dessus du second, et le dernier l'emporte sur tous*
> *les autres. L'action y est grande, complète; sa durée ne*
> *va point, ou fort peu, au delà de la représentation.*

It has at once beauty of subject, novelty of fiction,
force of verse, facility of expression, solidity of reasoning, warmth of passion, tenderness of love and friendship; and this happy assembly is handled so as to be
heightened from act to act. The second surpasses the
first, the third is above the second, and the last is
beyond all the others. Its action is great, complete;
its time-span does not go at all, or only a very little,
beyond that of the representation.

This census of desirable traits for a play stands, in itself, over
and to one side of the question of whether or not *Rodogune*
actually fulfills the claims made for it here.

In "la solidité du raisonnement," whatever their disposi-
tion to "la chaleur des passions," all the characters in a play
should participate. As it happens, no *solidité* leads the monu-
mentally evil mothers of *Rodogune* and *Théodore*, or the weak

and tyrannical fathers of *Théodore* and *Heraclius*, to question the value that centralizes the mounting progression of each action. In the falsified rigor of these late plays, the *empire* may be abused or thwarted but never transcended, while Racine's Titus and Bérénice and Antiochus, rulers one and all, carry away with them each to the throne of his own domain a value that renders the duty they are serving only a sorrowful negative qualification. Titus does homage to rule, and his idea about Rome remains Cornelian in its burden, though in its effects the play is *faussement cornélienne*, to adapt Charles Mauron's characterization.[63] Titus' summary, Cornelian in its internal solidity, subjects that Romanism to a sigh:

> *Rome me fit jurer de maintenir ses droits:*
> *Il les faut maintenir. Déjà plus d'une fois*
> *Rome a de mes pareils exercé la constance.*
> *Ah! si vous remontiez jusques à sa naissance,*
> *Vous les verriez toujours à ses ordres soumis.*
> *L'un, jaloux de sa foi, va chez les ennemis*
> *Chercher, avec la mort, la peine toute prête:*
> *D'un fils victorieux l'autre proscrit la tête;*
> *L'autre, avec des yeux secs et presque indifférents,*
> *Voit mourir ses deux fils par son ordre expirants.*
> (*Bérénice*, IV, 5)

> Rome had me swear on oath to uphold her rights:
> They must be upheld. Already more than once
> Rome has exercised the constancy of my peers.
> Ah! If you went as far back as her birth,
> You would see them always subject to her orders.
> One, jealous of his word, goes among enemies
> To seek, with his death, a punishment all ready:
> Another proscribes the head of a victor son;
> Another, with dry and almost indifferent eyes,
> Sees his two sons die, expiring on his orders.

Pour sortir des tourments dont mon âme est la proie,
Il est, vous le savez, une plus noble voie.
Je me suis vu, Madame, enseigner ce chemin
Et par plus d'un héros et par plus d'un Romain.

                                                    (V,6)

To leave the torments, to which my soul is prey,
There exists, as you know, a nobler way.
I saw myself, lady, being taught this path
By more than one hero and by more than one Roman.

The suicide threatened in the second of these quotations is an act of amorous desperation that no Roman or hero really teaches Titus. And the historical panorama of the first does not fill out the canvas of the *Bérénice* we are shown. The Cornelian value does not dominate and structure the action; it operates only as a negative internal commandment. The very openness of Racine's verses, the tendency discussed above for the second half of an alexandrine to diverge from the first, subverts them towards internal loss. The audience is asked to sympathize, not with the fulfillment of the last honor of empire, but with the greatness of the renunciation involved in acceding to it.

For Corneille the action evolves, as Doubrovsky says in writing of *Horace*, "dans la pure dialectique de Maîtrise... l'élargissement de la lutte solitaire des consciences aux dimensions collectives de l'histoire,"[64] though the *solitaire* and the *collective*, through the uniformity of the ideal, are only versions of one another (each perfectly definable in terms of the other), and *l'histoire* is present only in the form of an older generation, and not at all in the panorama of past power that Racine always opens up.

In one sense the person is subsistent, a convergence of an *être* and a *volonté*, to take the terms Poulet singles out.[65] His subsistence stands on the ever-patterned declaration of itself:

Je le suis, je veux l'être.

                                                    (*Cinna*, V,3)

Je sais ce que je suis.

                                                    (*Cid*, III,4)

Je sais ce que je dois, je sais ce que je puis.
                                                    (*Don Sanche*, I,1)

On the other hand, that subsistence measures itself not only against the most extreme commands of conflicting idealism, but in the context of the most centrally incorporated ideal, the royal authority. This authority is present over the play, since someone always possesses it; it is a future threatened in the play—it always has to be maintained by the heroic efforts of a Cinna or a Rodogune, an Heraclius or a Léontine.

The unity of that ideal launches the elevation of the couplets, the centripetal force of the action, and also the interconnections among the terms used to describe it. As Octave Nadal points out, *mérite, estime, devoir, vertu, générosité*, and *gloire* all depend on one another for definition.[66] To them can be added *amour*:

> *Cet amour épuré que Tite seul lui donne*
> *Renoncerait au rang pour être à la personne!*
> *Mais on a beau, Seigneur, raffiner sur ce point,*
> *La personne et le rang ne se séparent point.*
> > (*Tite et Bérénice*, V,2)

This purified love Titus alone gives her
Would renounce its rank to belong to her person!
But, lord, we would refine on this point in vain.
Person and rank may never separate.

Amour participates to such a degree in the other, public ideal that it includes its seeming opposites as traits:

La tendresse n'est point de l'amour d'un héros:
Il est honteux pour lui d'écouter des sanglots;
Et parmi la douceur des plus illustres flammes,
Un peu de dureté sied bien aux grandes âmes.

(Surena, V,4)

There is no tenderness in a hero's love:
It is shameful for him to listen to sobs;
And in the softness of the most illustrious flames,
A little hardness sits well with great souls.

This complex of ideas dominates his vision enough to survive into the later plays, from which these two quotations are taken, where it is no longer incorporated in the action. The logical possibility that faltering before the demands of nobility may lose love is presented only in the masquelike mythological trappings of *Andromède*, where the heroine turns from the quavering Phinée to the Persée who has saved her from the monster.

Upon like incredibilities does Corneille frame the extremeties of his plots after *Polyeucte*. The Christian heroism of forgiving the murder of a husband and a decade of persecution is exacted from a pre-Christian Rodogune. Prostitution, not death, is all but imposed on the martyr Théodore. In *Pulchérie* a queen whom honor keeps from marrying a subject who loves her, uses her royal authority to order him to marry an unloved rival and turns over the empire to him. Two suitors in *Attila* are asked by their tyrant-rival to fight a king's gladiatorial duel in public; the stalemate of their refusals finds only a miraculous issue in the massive hemorrhage that suddenly kills "the scourge of God." The hero of *Don Sanche* is asked to choose which of three declared suitors will marry the loving queen he loves. Eurydice poisons herself to die when her lover has died in *Surena*. On the side of empire, we are asked in *Heraclius* to believe that the noble Léontine would kill her own son to trick a tyrant, so that both the other infants in her care, the rightful emperor and the tyrant's son, might survive: and it still takes all the skill of the double agent Exupère to thread a veiled way to the throne of such absolute, but not dramatically absolutized, value—past the bewildering threats of two incests and one parricide along the way.

Corneille's sense of doubling his ideals, so beautifully poised in the balanced alexandrines and successive exactions of the major plays, here proliferates in a compulsion to provide every situation with a twin. Sophocles' *Oedipus* plot is not enough for his *Oedipe*, into which he builds a sister whose love for Thésée follows the vagaries of the mythic evolvement. Racine, in the *Bérénice* that came on the boards almost the same week as Corneille's *Tite et Bérénice,* restricts himself to just three principals. Corneille provides *his* Tite with a brother, whose mistress is ultimately married by Tite at the nobly sacrificing command of a Bérénice who heeds the Roman imperative forbidding Tite's marriage after Tite himself has wavered to propose to her.

At one point even the alexandrine is subverted; in the *Examen* of *Andromède*, Corneille is willing to condemn the Stances in the *Cid*, where they occur at only two points of pause, as "inexcusables"; then in *Agésilas* he inflates the regularity of his couplets into a series of crossed rhymes and varied lines. The bulk of dialogue in that play has been built into stanzas that can no more respond to the demands of progressive action than a series of pirouettes would get far in a hurdle race.

In his own way, and within his plays, Corneille seems to be overcome, as Racine was later, by the royal power. He ceases to examine that power, merely accepting it as a fatal value, in all the plays after *Théodore*, except perhaps for *Rodogune* and *Pertharite*. Even there the mastery of character and the austerity of incident merely hold in a kind of middle distance what the ideal nature of rule will be. The Grimoald of *Pertharite* is an Auguste who does not do more than assert the nobility which will make him transcend the horrors by which he attained power. He is not called on by the playwright to enact his *générosité*. His threat to kill Rodelinde's infant if she refuses him does not unify him into the amorous despair of Racine's Pyrrhus, whose similar gesture in *Andromaque* some suppose to have been borrowed from the older playwright. The dead hand of royal power is the underside of the moral extravagance in all these plays. These excesses are covering in the action for an automatism of royal idolatry. The ground is no longer live, the power has withdrawn from enactment.

The deplorable defection of Corneille's later career is simple enough to be put in a formula—and this formula, unlike the formula of Racine, cannot serve as the diagram for an enacted ideal. The formula for Corneille's late plays produces only the illusion of an ideal: lovers suffering under an unjust or usurped or vacillating royal authority, which may also participate in the love as a rival, find that the complications of court intrigue exact from them a temporary or permanent renunciation of love (*Rodogune, Heraclius, Don Sanche, Nicomède, Pertharite, Sertorius, Sophonisbe, Othon, Agésilas, Attila, Tite et Bérénice, Pulchérie, Surena*). The formulaic oversimplicity of this late series remains unbroken, except by the facile mythologizing of *Andromède, Oedipe,* and *La Conquête de la Toison d'Or.*

4

The psychological roots of the theatre derive from the danger investing the taboo that we should not look at the doings of others. We should either have an assigned part or absent ourselves: the social circle is always total. Theatre imposes a paradoxical convention on that totality by providing a space where we do watch: the totality of the social circle is presumed to allow an openness that violates its essential condition. The theater harnesses the danger, and awakens questioning about sexuality (characteristically in comedy) and mortality (characteristically in tragedy) by transmitting a coherent action into a language that, through the convention, allays the danger it har-

nesses and lulls the questions it awakens. The powerful causal
series in a play converts the emotion attendant on the danger,
and on the extraordinary ritual-analogies inherent in the convention, to transmit the immediate sense of possible coherent
totality for the restricted society on stage.

In faithful Renaissance fashion, Corneille, like Shakespeare,
begins to speak in public of that which is normally kept silent
and unobserved out of deference to the taboo on the primal
scene: he writes comedies about love. Lovers in real life exclude
from all the direct and oedipal dangers those who might be idle
auditors; they do this by staying silent about love, by being
quiet when more than the devoted pair are present; three's a
crowd. But the lovers on stage do speak; the audience crowd is
a third. Breaking the taboo overwhelms the auditor at the same
time that the stage convention keeps him from being over-
whelmed. The stage convention sublimates the voyeur in the
spectator, and the volatile amorous propensities of the charged
theatrical medium are released, "tragically," in the real life
of that new Renaissance phenomenon, the actress.

An audience will go away from any idle love comedy with
some charged enlivening of sensibility. Racine destroys that
idleness by tightening it into a totality, by making it tragic
and mortal: the charged enlivening in the power of enactment
becomes a sorrowing intimation of ordered existence. What the
idealized sexuality of his protoganists goes under to is the most
complex, and also the most unified, form of organization
against mortality: imperial rule. When he writes, he melts the
empire into the dominance of love, while Corneille, at his peak,
balances the two together in a straining vision that he is still
able to describe when he is past his powers, towards the end of
the *Examen* of *Nicomède*:

> *Dans l'admiration qu'on a pour sa vertu, je trouve une*
> *manière de purger les passions dont n'a point parlé*
> *Aristote et qui est peut-être plus sure que celle qu'il*
> *prescrit à la tragédie par le moyen de la pitié et de la*
> *crainte. L'amour qu'elle nous donne pour cette vertu*

que nous admirons, nous imprime de la haine pour le vice contraire. La grandeur de courage de Nicomède nous laisse une aversion de la pusillanimité; et la généreuse reconnaissance d'Héraclius, qui expose sa vie pour Martian, à qui il est redevable de la sienne, nous jette dans l'horreur de l'ingratitude.

In the admiration for his virtue, I find a manner of purging the passions about which Aristotle has not spoken at all—one that is perhaps surer than that which he prescribes for tragedy through the means of pity and fear. The love it gives us for the virtue we admire impresses hate in us for the contrary vice. The grandeur of Nicomède's courage leaves with us an aversion for pusillanimity; and the large-hearted recognition of Heraclius, who exposes his life for Martian, to whom he owes his own, throws us into horror before ingratitude.

This puts in allopathic, negative terms, what, without accepting his specific examples from the failed late play, we may see also in a positive light. What Boileau described, in a letter to Perrault as the "sublimité" of Corneille, may also be opposed, as Boileau opposes it, to the "pitié" and "terreur" of Aristotle.[67] Enacted virtue may have also a homeopathic contagion; to the end of that sublimity, pity and terror are only instruments, for any enactment that has power. And the contagion need only be apprehended for the enactment to transmit its power: it is a message that, like all messages, has something of an imperative built into its purified transcendences.

5

The will of a person is inextricably involved in the existential dynamics of time, in the process of reflectively and reflexively mediating a past situation, one that will have come to a head in a supple complex of present imperatives. The will mediates itself into a future that is always in the process of becoming what the present has made of the past. Consequently the will only preponderates towards the finality of self-realization (grace and virtue) or self-condemnation (fault; the nonrealization of nothingness). A classic tragedy sets finality at the outset, by the convention of tautening ("unifying") the causality of the action in space and time. It gives the future the attributes of the past and the present by ironing out all three; and it makes the future as definite as only the presented past can be.

The power of such an enactment, by thus annulling the difference between past and future, reverses the conditions of life when it seems only to be heightening them (and thereby also heightening them to a maximum). All qualities do possess their defects. And peoples' defects, through the full effect of a tight dramatic causality, become radical faults. The taut action of a play dramatizes the preponderances of interactive wills by miming, from the initial conception and the first raising of the curtain, what in actuality can only be a result. In this sense, of envisioning possibilities while radicalizing faults, all tragedies are Christian.

For these very reasons—because of the logical shifts necessarily involved in the tight convention of putting a play on in the first place—a tragedy cannot have people within it who are directly espousing Christian ideals. The tangent must be found, if the playwright is Christian, of potentiality (the Rome of Corneille[68] and Racine) or of silent assumption (Corneille edits the devotional effusions out of his source for the *Cid*), of stripped desire (Racine), or exaltation through the conflict of imperatives (Corneille). All these solutions are tenser and tidier than Shakespeare's casuistic checks-and-balances in *Measure for Measure*, his fairytale resolution in *Merchant of Venice* (both comedies that express some tragic overtone), his melding of Christian imperatives with familial and political struggle in *Hamlet*, to go no further in his career.

For Corneille and Racine, the central power of their enactment is splendidly their own, incomparably single in its effect
and apparent in its presentation. For them the tightening of
the future into the attributes of the past is enacted at such a
pitch that the radical fault in the enacted universe finds no
flaw within a character where it may specially lodge: these
plays, in adopting "Aristotelian" unities, are thus trans-Aristo-
telian, purer and simpler dramas than anyone with the Greeks
alone before him could have imagined.

NOTES

1. Erving Goffman, *Frame Analysis* (New York, 1974). Framing could be described as a ritualization, nascent or residual.
2. René Girard, "'To Entrap the Wisest': A Reading of *The Merchant of Venice*" in Edward W. Said, ed., *Literature and Society* (Baltimore: The Johns Hopkins University Press, 117). An elaboration of the system from which this aphorism is drawn has been offered in *Des Choses cachées depuis la fondation du monde* (Paris, 1979).
3. R.C. Knight, in *Racine* (London, 1969, p. 19), points out the force of the special metrical wrench in this line: "We realize now the explosive emotion indicated in the last line of *Bérénice* ...though we can never feel it as we should; because no one now would shrink, as every poet did then, from placing an *adieu* or an *hélas* in the second hemistich."
4. Gordon Pocock, in *Corneille and Racine*, (Cambridge, 1973) discusses the complexities that Racine and Corneille brought to bear on questions relating to the unities. See also Jacques Schérer, *La Dramaturgie classique en France* (Paris, 1950).
5. Raymond Picard, *La Carrière de Jean Racine* (Paris, 1956), p. 86.
6. Lucien Goldmann, *Racine* (Paris, 1956).
7. Jean Duvignaud, *L'Acteur* (Paris, 1965).
8. Charles Mauron, *L'Inconscient dans l'oeuvre et la vie de Racine* (Gap, 1957).
9. Some aspects of this contrast are discussed in Maurice Delcroix, *Le Sacré dans les tragédies profanes de Racine* (Paris, 1970).
10. Michel Butor, *Répertoire* I, (Paris, 1960), pp. 28–61.
11. Roland Barthes, *Sur Racine* (Paris, 1963), p.78.
12. Lucien Goldmann, *Le Dieu caché* (Paris, 1955), p. 50.
13. Albert Cook, *The Classic Line* (Bloomington, 1966), Chapter IV. R.A. Sayce ("Racine's Style: Periphrasis and Direct Statement" in R.C. Knight, *Racine*, 132–146) finds the effect of this style, as it presents itself, to hold both periphrasis and direct statement in a sort of balance.
14. Mauron, *L'Inconscient dans l'oeuvre*, p. 75.
15. John Lapp, "Racine's Symbolism", in R.C. Knight, *Racine*, pp. 65–74.

16. Goldmann, *Le Dieu caché*, p. 369.

17. Louis Racine, "Mémoires contenant quelques particularités sur la vie et les ouvrages de Jean Racine," in Jean Racine, *Oeuvres Complètes*, (Pléiade: Paris, 1950), I, pp. 30–32.

18. As Theophil Spoerri says ("Racine: Impulse and Mind", in R.C. Knight, *Racine*, pp. 49–64) p. 58, "The obscure pressure of elemental impulses is felt all the more threateningly since it is these that violently remove one human being from his conscious and controlled relationship to another. Mind is the connecting, committing and binding factor." We may still not follow Spoerri in the strong opposition he sets up between these two internal forces, since the onmipresent nobility in the best characters offers the example of their fusion.

19. Goldmann, *Le Dieu caché*, pp. 348–352.

20. Goldmann, *Racine*. The point is repeated in *Le Dieu caché*, p. 351.

21. Picard, *La Carrière*, pp. 417–433.

22. Jean Duvignaud, *Sociologie du théatre* (Paris, 1965).

23. Mauron, *L'Inconscient dans l'oeuvre*, pp. 294-301.

24. Irving Feldman, in a communication to the author.

25. Mauron, *L'Inconscient dans l'oeuvre*, pp. 298-299.

26. Lionel Abel, *Metatheatre* (New York, 1963).

27. Goldmann, *Le Dieu caché*, p. 351. The italics are Goldmann's.

28. "Epithaphe de M. Arnauld," *Oeuvres*, II, p. 185.

29. Picard, *La Carrière*, p. 478.

30. Mauron, *L'Inconscient das l'oeuvre*, p. 74.

31. In a letter of 16 March 1672, as cited in Paul Bénichou, *Morales du Grande Siècle* (Paris, 1948), p. 13.

32. Lucien Goldmann, *Recherches dialectiques* (Paris, 1959), p. 91. *Le Dieu caché*, pp. 337-440.

33. Aligned with Corneille by Gustave Lanson, "Le Héros cornélien et le 'Généreux,'" *Revue d'histoire littéraire*, 1894, pp. 397–411, as cited by Bénichou, p. 25.

34. Picard, *La Carrière*, pp. 95-98.

35. Cited in Martin Turnell, *The Classical Moment* (London, n.d.), p. 133.

36. Georges Poulet, *Études sur le temps humain* (Paris, 1950), pp. 105-106.

37. *Ibid.*, p. 120.

38. Mauron, *L'Inconscient dans l'oeuvre*, p. 99.

39. Charles Baudouin, *Jean Racine l'enfant du désert* (Paris, 1963), p. 95.

40. Mauron, *L'Inconscient dans l'oeuvre*, p. 28.
41. Baudouin, p. 41, citing Daniel Mornet, *Jean Racine* (Paris, 1944).
42. Underlined by the editor Raymond Picard in *Oeuvres*, I, p. 233.
43. Bénichou, *Morales*, p. 28, p. 30.
44. Barthes, *Sur Racine*, p. 20.
45. Albert Cook, *Prisms* (Bloomington, 1967), Chapter V.
46. Leo Spitzer, *Linguistics and Literary History* (Princeton, 1948), p. 91.
47. *Ibid.*, p. 110.
48. Ernst Cassirer, *Descartes, Corneille, Christine du Suède* (Paris, 1942), p. 9.
49. *Ibid.*, p. 12.
50. Along these lines, Jean Starobinski makes a point that would coordinate the mutual perceptions of the characters with the logical break of the verse ("The Poetics of the Glance in Racine," in R.C. Knight, *Racine*, pp. 88–100): "The hero's energy of will is enhanced by a second force, that of the admiring glances turned upon him in surrender. The Corneillian *event* occurs at the meeting of these two. Moreover the hero knows implicitly that he is seen exactly as he shows himself, neither diminished nor deformed. ...In Racine the importance of the glance is not less, but its value and meaning are entirely different. It is a glance lacking not intensity but fullness, unable to hold the object in steady view. The act of seeing, for Racine, remains forever haunted by tragedy."
51. *Oevres*, Vol. I, p. 42. "...quand il entreprenait und tragédie, il disposait chaque acte en prose. Quand il avait ainsi lié toutes les scènes entre elles, il disait: Ma tragédie est faite, comptant le reste pour rien." [We may well doubt, of course, the interpretation of the last phrase while accepting the accuracy of the description.] For Corneille, see Georges May, *Tragédie corneillienne, tragédie racinienne* (Urbana, 1948), p. 224.
52. May, *Tragédie corneillienne*, p. 155.
53. *Ibid.*, p. 255.
54. Octave Nadal, *L'Amour dans l'oeuvre de Pierre Corneille* (Paris, 1963), p. 127.
55. Serge Doubrovsky, *Corneille et la dialectique du héros* (Paris, 1963), p. 127.
56. Cassirer, p. 9.
57. Jean Rousset, *Forme et signification*, Paris, 1964, pp. 7–16.
58. Cassirer, *Descartes, Corneille, Christine du Suède*, p. 18.
59. Doubrovsky, *Corneille*, p. 149.

60. *Ibid.*, p. 87.
61. Leo Lowenthal, *Literature and the Image of Man* (Boston, 1957), Chapter on the *Cid*.
62. Doubrovsky, *Corneille*, p. 91.
63. Mauron, *L'Inconscient dans l'oeuvre*, p. 86.
64. Doubrovsky, *Corneille*, p. 149.
65. Poulet, *Études*, p. 92.
66. Nadal, *L'Amour*, pp. 286-321.
67. May, *Tragédie corneilliene*, p. 23.
68. That there was a difficulty in such presentation is indicated by the resistance Corneille encountered to the *Cid*. As one contemporary said of *Polyeucte*, "Y-a-t-il personne qui ne soit mille fois plus touché de l'affliction de Sévère lorsqu'il trouve Pauline mariée que du martyre de Polyeucte? ...aussi Dieu n'a pas choisi le théâtre pour y faire éclater la gloire de ses martyrs; il ne l'a pas choisi pour y instruire ceux qu'il appelle à la participation de son héritage." Prince de Conti, *Traité de la comédie*, 1666, pp. 36-37, as cited in Georges Mongrédien, ed., *Recueil des textes et des documents du XVIIᵉ siècle relatifs à Corneille* (Paris, 1972); with other comparable strictures, pp. 98-101.